MORE PRAISE FOR

# The Insiders Guide to the Best Jobs on Bay Street

"An extremely useful and relevant guide to careers in the Canadian investment industry. The book combines detailed job descriptions with real world tips and insights from industry practitioners to provide a complete picture of Bay Street's major job categories. This book is strongly recommended for people seeking employment on the Street."
> —*Joseph Sirdevan, CFA, Director of Research,*
> *Jarislowsky Fraser Ltd.*

"Joe Kan's book provides an excellent insight into the various opportunities in the financial world, what it takes to get there, and what's involved once you've arrived. Those of you looking for jobs in the investment industry are well-served by Joe's research and insights into the different parts of this fascinating business."
> —*Patrick O'Toole, CFA, and President of the*
> *Toronto Society of Financial Analysts*

"This book provides an insider's look at the competitive world of the investment business and is a valuable resource for anyone pursuing or considering a career on Bay Street."
> —*Daniel Muzyka, Dean of the Sauder School of Business and*
> *RBC Financial Group Professor of Entrepreneurship, The*
> *University of British Columbia*

# ABOUT THE AUTHOR

JOE KAN, CFA, is a headhunter based in Toronto, Canada. His practice (www.theheadhunter.ca) is focused on recruiting professionals in institutional equity sales, trading, research, and investment banking. Prior to founding the firm, he worked as an equity research associate at a mid-sized investment dealer and then in institutional sales at a couple of independent boutiques. He holds a Bachelor of Commerce from the University of Windsor. He is the editor of the best-selling two-volume *Handbook of Canadian Security Analysis*, also published by John Wiley & Sons.

# the insiders guide to the
# BEST
# JOBS
## on BAY Street

# the insiders guide to the

# BEST JOBS on BAY Street

## Joe Kan, CFA

John Wiley & Sons Canada, Ltd.

**National Library of Canada Cataloguing in Publication Data**

Kan, Joe
        The insiders guide to the best jobs on Bay
Street / Joe Kan.

ISBN 0-470-83528-1

        1. Finance--Vocational guidance--Ontario--Toronto.
2. Financial institutions--Vocational guidance--Ontario--Toronto.
3. Business--Vocational guidance--Ontario--Toronto.
4. Bay Street (Toronto, Ont.)  I. Title.

HG5154.3.K35 2005        332'.023'713541        C2004-906891-1


**Production Credits**
Cover: Kyle Gell Design
Interior text design: Interrobang Graphic Design Inc.
Printer: Transcontinental Printing

John Wiley & Sons Canada, Ltd
6045 Freemont Boulevard
Mississauga, Ontario
L5R 4J3

Printed in Canada
10 9 8 7 6 5 4 3 2 1

# Contents

*Foreword by Andrew Willis*     ix

*Acknowledgements*     xv

*Introduction*     1

**Chapter 1**:     Research Associate     5

**Chapter 2**:     Sell-Side Equity Analyst     27

**Chapter 3**:     Institutional Equity Sales     65

**Chapter 4**:     Institutional Equity Trader     93

**Chapter 5**:     Investment Banker     121

**Chapter 6**:     Equity Capital Markets Professional     153

**Chapter 7**:     Venture Capitalist     179

**Chapter 8**:     Portfolio Manager     209

**Chapter 9**:     Hedge Fund Manager     245

# Foreword

BY ANDREW WILLIS

I WALKED OUT OF UNIVERSITY holding a degree that I've since lost track of and a bright orange scrapbook that's still kicking around my basement.

The book is filled with carefully clipped job advertisements, all for positions of one sort or another in finance. I incurred the wrath of librarians everywhere by chopping up *The Economist* to get ads for World Bank jobs in Africa. Stockbroker slots at firms long gone bust or bought by banks filled page after page. I pasted in tiny recruitment spots that offered positions in Toronto for analysts at debt-rating agencies. I can't imagine what I would have done if someone had actually interviewed me and asked what a bond was.

My diligence in clipping ads, mailing in resumés, and recording all my follow-up phone calls by date, name of the oh-so-polite receptionist, and next planned call was only surpassed by my complete lack of knowledge about the jobs I was applying for.

My whole experience with the stock market could be summed up in one late-afternoon trip to the visitor's gallery above the old Toronto Stock Exchange, where I saw a few paunchy guys in bad sports jackets, chatting wearily at the end of the day. The business section of the newspaper was just a roadblock on the way to sports.

Yet my dream was to be a research analyst at a big brokerage house. Just what an analyst researched was totally beyond me. They analyzed. That sounded great. Big thinking, 30,000-foot stuff. Six-figure salary, and plenty of expensive scotch after work. For that matter, I didn't really know what a brokerage house brokered.

Nor did I spend a whole lot of time considering whether I had the necessary toolbox to be an analyst—this despite the fact that accounting remained a dark, mysterious art through several years of higher education, even with the best attempts of my professors.

Well, over time, the scrapbook filled up with a fairly impressive collection of rejection letters. The World Bank used an extremely fine paper stock to tell me to please go away. I started selling advertising to pay down student debts, but kept plugging away for a spot on the Street. Then, a friend who had a roommate dating a woman at a recruiting firm threw me a tip. One of the biggest investment dealers, then known as Wood Gundy, needed an assistant in its research department.

I bought a new red tie. I made it through two rounds of interviews without once having to discuss LIFO, FIFO, or any other completely baffling accounting issue. I got the job. I was told to report for work at 7 in the morning. It was a struggle, but I managed to arrive on the first day by 6:45. To my shock, I found the department was already full of people, all working flat out. And there wasn't a scotch bottle in sight.

Until you have felt the energy of a large equity desk, and an equally large research department, all feeding fuel into a roaring bull market, you can't imagine the crackle in the air. This was the mid-1980s. The crash of '87 was still miles up the road.

I knew enough to know that all around me, every single morning, seriously smart people were making, and losing, enormous pots of money. I knew enough to realize that the analysts whose reports I edited, and the salesmen that I handed those reports to, were crackerjack quick—faster on their feet than anyone I'd ever met before. And I knew enough to know I was in way, way over my head.

I bailed out. I retreated to school and took up journalism. I ended up writing about the people I once worked with.

Today, working at an investment dealer isn't quite such a mystery, though I'm still hazy on the whole LIFO and FIFO thing. Through three bull markets, including the incredible tech bubble, and two brutal bears, I've enjoyed watching the best in the business strut their stuff, and I've seen some complete idiots crash.

For bright, ambitious people, there is simply no arena like the stock market. It's high-octane energy, mind-blowing wins, and gut wrenching losses every single day you come to work. For the dim but persistent, it's also a damn fine place to make a living.

The best of the analysts I so admired possess a cold familiarity with the numbers. The great traders and sellers of stocks and bonds blend their math skills with a gift of the gab. Deal-making investment bankers command all the skills of great generals, and like the senior officers they can win a battle, then leave the field to others who must win the peace.

But standout as they may be at the peak of their careers, many professionals (including the individuals profiled in this book) were likely equally ignorant of what plays out on the Street when they first started their careers.

Bringing it all together is Joe Kan, a headhunter who has poached more talent in the institutional equity business than any of his competitors. His knack for pulling together some of the best in the business to participate in his ventures is again reflected in the all-star line-up in this book. He has interviewed professionals from a variety of backgrounds. The achievements of each, their standing in the community, and sterling reputations, offer an example of what it takes to be successful and respected in an intense, competitive world.

When it comes to doing deals, no one has turned more in the past decade than Wayne Adlam, the head of equity capital markets at CIBC World Markets. He and his team work with both companies and investors to structure financings, and they can count pioneering work in income trusts and cross-border stock sales among their many accomplishments.

Tatiana Badescu has made her mark in the emerging world of private equity, a sector that's got the attention of every institutional investor. Over the past five years, she's worked at the venture capital arm of Royal Bank of Canada and at Vengrowth, the largest Canadian venture capital fund.

Judy Blumstock has been on the cutting edge of bio-tech. She's parlayed a biology degree and Columbia MBA into health sciences financing work at Royal Bank, and now as a principal at Genesys Capital Partners, an early-stage venture capital player.

Another doer-of-deals on an equity capital markets desk is Marilia Costa, an expert in small-cap companies by virtue of her perch at Orion Securities. She's packaged up hundreds of tech and resource stocks in her tenure at the employee-owned brokerage house.

The head of sales at the busiest equity desk in Canada is David Fleck, at BMO Nesbitt Burns. He's been a top-ranked salesman, helping portfolio managers understand the market, and is now the well-regarded head of the team that moves more blocks of stocks than anyone else in the country.

One of the industry's up-and-comers is Mason Granger, who is in the trenches as a senior research associate at RBC Capital Markets. He's building off a chemical engineering background, and has been fortunate enough to have worked for three top-ranked stock analysts during the last three years.

When it comes to cross-border experience, few can match the wisdom of Steve Garmaise. He's been the head of research at both Merrill Lynch and RBC Capital Markets, working in Canada and the United States, during a period of enormous upheaval for analysts. Steve was also a top-ranked special situations analyst at several dealers before moving into management.

Among the mutual fund stars, few burn brighter than Keith Graham. He has made money for investors in good markets and bad while picking stocks at some of the country's biggest mutual funds, including those of current employer AGF Management and arch-rival AIM Trimark.

One of the first calls that many portfolio managers make each morning goes to Kelly Gray, an anchor on the top-notch sales team at RBC Capital Markets for the past decade. Equally experienced is Glen Grossmith, a trader for 20 years, with stints on the most productive desks on the Street, including Gordon Capital, First Marathon, and now UBS Securities.

Andrea Horan has consistently won plaudits for her calls on media and cable stocks, and has experienced both bank-ownership and the entrepreneurial challenges of owning a firm during stints with RBC Capital Markets, Westwind Partners, and now Genuity Capital Partners. Another strong up-and-comer to the community is Aaron Lau, a graduate of the revered University of British Columbia's portfolio management program, and currently an investment banking associate at TD Securities.

After cashing out by selling the mutual fund he co-founded, Jim McGovern has re-invented himself as one of Canada's hedge fund leaders by starting Arrow Hedge Partners. When it comes to doing deals in Canada, and outside our border, Pat Meneley has seen it all as an investment banker with American powerhouse Salomon Brothers, and now as head of corporate finance at TD Securities.

Another convert to the hedge fund cause is Tom Schenkel. He paid his dues as an equity research associate, then was quickly promoted to special situations analyst, which in turn proved to be a stepping-stone to co-founding hedge fund Epic Capital. And we've got insights from Dave Vanderwood, who cut his teeth at venture capital firm

Cavendish Investing, before becoming an analyst, then leaving the sell-side to become a portfolio manager at market leader Burgundy Asset Management.

These individuals are all living the jobs I pasted into that orange scrapbook so many years ago—jobs that contain the potential for adventures far more satisfying, and a lot more fun, than anything I'd ever imagined. Hopefully, this book will open up a door to that world.

# ACKNOWLEDGEMENTS

To both the professionals that allowed me a formal interview for publication, as well as the following, who gave generously of their feedback and time. Without any one of their thoughts, this book would certainly be worse off. Without all of them, this book would not have been completed at all.

I would like to gratefully acknowledge the following for their contributions: Wayne Adlam, Simon Akit, William Aldridge, Jaret Anderson, Peter Angelou, Tom Antony, Steve Arpin, Tatiana Badescu, Casey Baker, Dana Benner, Geoff Bertram, Craig Bethune, Ali Bhojani, Judy Blumstock, Tim Brown, Ben Cherniavsky, Doran Chernichen, Kelvin Cheung, Adelaide Chiu, Brian Clouse, Marilia Costa, David Fleck, Pierre Fournier, Margaret Franklin, Steve Garmaise, Barbara Glassford, Andrew Gordon, Keith Graham, Mason Granger, Kelly Gray, Steve Green, Glen Grossmith, Robert Heinkel, Jim Hinds, Grant Hofer, Andrea Horan, Patrick Horan, Horst Hueniken, Kathy Jeramz-Larson, Jill Kasner, Tom Kehoe, Freeda Khan, Daniel Kim, Craig King, Wally Kusters, Michael Lam, Alan Lane, Frederick Larkin, Aaron Lau, Mike Lerner, Michael Letros, John Paul Lotesto, Greg Macdonald, James MacDonald, David MacNaughtan, Mary Ann Madore, Steve Mantel, Jim McGovern, Nirvaan Meharchand, Pat Meneley, Allan Meyer, Greg Milavsky, Menal Patel, Bill Peckford, Ed Peplinski, Shant Poladian,

Steve Rawn, Greg Reid, Peter Rockandel, Alex Sasso, Tom Schenkel, Rod Sim, Matt Skipp, John Smolinkski, David Smyth, Tim Snelgrove, Michelle Soon-Shiong, Paul Steep, Duncan Stewart, Jamie Stiff, Bruce Tatters, Greg Thompson, David Vanderwood, Mary Vitug, Stephen Watson, Craig Webster, Aleksander Weiler, Macmurray Whale, Ewart White, Kevin Williams, and Rick Wilson.

To the staff at Wiley, thank you for taking on yet another book project with me and for your patience throughout the process.

To my friend and former colleague David Smyth, I would like to extend a long overdue thanks for not giving me grief after I used one of his proprietary charts in my first book (*Handbook of Canadian Security Analysis, Volume 1*), neither having asked his permission nor given him proper credit.

# INTRODUCTION

IT IS NOT UNCOMMON TO SEE some of the best and brightest from other professions make the career switch over to the Bay Street* investment community to take advantage of their peak earning years. Young pharmacists and doctors go to business school to become healthcare/biotech analysts, and successful corporate/securities lawyers make the switch to investment banking and mergers and acquisitions. The funny thing though, is that you don't see successful healthcare/biotech analysts applying to medical school to become pharmacists or doctors. Nor do you see investment bankers looking to switch into corporate or securities law. The simple reason is this: next to pro sports and rock stars, no other career compensates its players as well for their efforts as does the meritocracy-based culture of the Bay Street investment community.

The community, however, is a tough one to break into. The competition for jobs is fierce. And everything you've ever heard about the huge hours and the huge egos are true, but so are the huge rewards (both financial and intellectual) that await you if you pay your dues—work hard, do more than is asked, and put in your time.

---

\* The term Bay Street is used throughout the book to refer to the institutional investment community in Canada as a whole and not *only* to the Toronto community that the term suggests.

The first few years in the business are an opportunity whereby you are essentially being paid to learn. Nonetheless, the first few years in an entry-level role can be demanding. Research associates put in 60–80 hour workweeks, while investment banking analysts put in 80–100 hour workweeks. And while doing so they're studying for their Chartered Financial Analyst (CFA) exams. A simple calculation (the bi-weekly paycheque divided by hours worked) puts you back at the same hourly wage as in your high school days when you were flipping burgers.

But they do it for a reason—the potential to make a lot of money. (In other professions like accounting and law, however, the unfortunate reality is that there are a finite number of billable hours.) This is a business where the stars can make well into the seven figures in their peak earning years, and the mediocre can still make upwards of half a million bucks a year (or more!). And let's not kid ourselves, if your career motives were more altruistic, you wouldn't have picked up this book. You would have picked up a book titled something like *An Insiders Guide to Making the World a Better Place*.

So who makes it in the business and who doesn't? As best as I can tell, the winning formula for success on Bay Street is one part talent, one part ambition, one part work ethic, and one part personality.

Some minimum level of talent is required but talent alone won't cut it. Many extremely bright individuals don't make it. Go stand at the corner of King and Bay Streets and look around at the gleaming office towers. There's an awful lot of bright people working in those buildings but very few are making north of half a million dollars by the time they hit their early 30s.

And while being personable alone won't do it either, personality is key since the investment business is essential-ly a service business. Furthermore, the investment business is one where you sell intangible products, so people skills and the ability to communicate are valued higher than in other businesses where the potential client can "kick the tires" of your product(s). And most importantly, being personable is important simply because people (clients) won't talk to you if they don't like you.

So once you're in the business, here's how it plays out:

In your mid-20s, you get into the business and take the first few years to learn the industry. At this stage, the name and brand equity of the firm on your business card is relatively more important than at any other time in your career.

In your early 30s, you're building your personal franchise—both reputation and transportable client relationships.

In your mid-30s to early 40s, you are likely in your peak earning years. At this stage, your personal franchise is established and the name of the firm on your business card is less relevant. This is typically the stage where seasoned professionals look to get equity in a firm to leverage their personal franchise, by either joining an independent boutique or getting involved with starting one up. As a senior investment banker friend of mine has suggested, "If you're not the lead dog, the view's all the same."

As a headhunter whose practice has been focused solely on the institutional investment community, I've noticed that many smart, business-minded individuals from MBA school and other professions looking to break into the business know surprisingly little about the career options on Bay Street. And just as important, they know little about the responsibilities and expectations of those options. And certainly people outside the investment community don't appreciate the hard work, sacrifices, and the nuances of the Street's pecking order.

My favourite story that illustrates the above point: A young guy I know busted his butt through MBA school to land a good job on Bay Street. Upon graduation, he got hired into one of the top bank-owned investment dealers** in Canada as a research associate. Never mind the cache of working at one of the top firms, he also happens to score a spot working for the #1-ranked analyst in his sector. And not to mention that this young guy is putting in 14-hour days *and* studying for his CFA! So upon meeting his girlfriend's mother, he mentions that he works at CIBC World Markets. All she hears (and remembers) is "CIBC". At the wedding shortly afterwards, the new mother-in-law approaches him and says, "Oh, how's it going? Which branch of the bank is it that you work at again? I keep meaning to stop in and say hello!" Talk about getting no respect!

And due to this lack of insight, a good number of the professionals on Bay Street did not consciously choose the "best job" in which they ultimately landed. As luck and circumstance would have it, they fell upon the role and excelled.

This book is written in the hopes that job seekers who are remotely interested in the investment arena now have a resource with which to assess the best opportunities themselves and not leave their career/future to luck or circumstance.

And perhaps once you've landed one of the best jobs on Bay Street, you may want to pass this book over to your mother-in-law.

---

** The terms brokerage firm, investment bank, and investment dealer are used interchangeably throughout this book.

# 1

# Research
# ASSOCIATE

# CHAPTER 1

# Research Associate

## Overview

THE RESEARCH ASSOCIATE (also known as *associate analyst*) job is the classic entry-level position and training opportunity on Bay Street. More institutional equity professionals and money managers have launched their careers from this position than any other.

Research associates work directly under a senior equity analyst, mainly building financial models, conducting industry and company research, and assisting in the writing and preparation of research comments/reports. They essentially free up a senior analyst's time so that the senior analyst can focus on activities that generate revenue or build his or her franchise (e.g., communicating time-sensitive information or trade ideas to institutional clients and the institutional sales/trading desk, performing quarterly client visits, etc.).

The typical tenure of an associate is two to three years. However, Bay Street continues to be a meritocracy, and therefore career progression is highly correlated to personal performance and the timing of opportunities. After serving as an associate, most associates move into institutional equity sales/trading, investment banking, or money management, or they get promoted to an analyst position. It is not uncommon to see associates leave their own firm in order to make the next step up. The old adage "You gotta move out to move up" still rings true.

Associates are typically assigned to a specific industry sector, or one of the investment strategy, economics, or quantitative research teams.

"The role of a research associate is simply to make his or her senior analyst look good."
—*Mike Letros, CFA, Institutional Equity Sales, Putnam Lovell NBF*

### Education

There was a time not too long ago when all you needed for a research associate position was an undergraduate degree in business/commerce and a good handshake. Now, few candidates without an MBA or CA are even considered. And for the purposes of recruiting research associates, I don't believe that the university a candidate graduates from is as important to Canadian investment dealers as superior academic performance and relevant summer work experience. (It's different in the United States where an MBA from one of the top 10 business schools would definitely offer a competitive advantage.)

There are a couple of industry sectors where candidates should have a more technical academic background. More often than not, research associates in the health care/biotech sector have some kind of health sciences undergraduate and/or master's degree (biochemistry, pharmacology, etc.), and associates in the mining sector have an earth sciences background (geology, mineral exploration, etc.). Candidates without these backgrounds have been hired as associates in those sectors and they've managed to do a good job. However, if one's intention is to graduate into an analyst role in one of these industry sectors, not having the specialized background tends to limit upward mobility. When a mining exploration company's prospects are based on the results of one drill hole or an emerging biotech company's prospects are based on evaluating early Phase II clinical trials, an analyst needs to have the technical background to have credibility.

### Compensation Range

There are five main factors that determine individual compensation at the associate level:

1. **The overall equity business volumes.** The volume of equity business and the resulting profitability of brokerage firms are the prime determinants of industry compensation levels (and employment levels)

2. **The industry sector.** An associate analyst working in a "hot" sector (one where investor interest is driving up the stock values and trading volumes,) will likely get a better bonus than one working in a sector where there is little or no investor interest

3. **Personal performance.** Just work hard, deliver more than is asked for, and hope for the best

4. **Seniority.** All things being equal, associates can expect a better bonus in year two and even better in year three

5. **The type of firm.** Global and U.S. dealers tend to pay at the higher end of the range. But given that the majority (more than 90%) of research associate jobs on Bay Street are those at the domestic firms, it is more realistic to expect annual comp at the lower to middle spectrum of the range ($70,000 to $110,000).

## Industry Certification

In 1959, the Institute of Chartered Financial Analysts (ICFA) was formed. In June 1963, the first CFA charters were handed out. In 1990, the ICFA merged with the Financial Analysts Federation (FAF) to become the Association of Investment Management and Research (AIMR).

AIMR changed its name in 2004 to CFA Institute, to reflect its role as administrator of the Chartered Financial Analyst (CFA) program. The program covers topics such as corporate finance, economics, portfolio management, and financial statement analysis.

To earn the CFA charter, a CFA candidate must pass 3 six-hour examinations over at least two years (CFA Institute suggests that 250 hours of study is needed to prepare for each exam) and have spent three years working in a role where he or she is involved in the investment decision-making process.

The average pass rate for each of the exams tends to hover around 50%. Of the 56,000 CFA charterholders worldwide, few have passed all three exams consecutively.

Having the CFA designation is highly recommended. The CFA designation has become the standard in the investment/finance industry. The program may or may not make you a better stock picker, but successful completion of the program has become a rite of passage into the institutional investment community. Most research directors prefer to see candidates who have obtained the designation or are making progress towards completing the program.

## Getting Started

Getting your *first* job on Bay Street is a challenge to most job-seekers, but once you land a position, getting your next one should be simpler.

Few research departments recruit on college/university campuses. Research staff are usually hired on an "as needed" basis. Most research bosses prefer to hire pre-trained candidates for immediate productivity.

There are several ways of securing an associate job on the sell-side (listed from easiest to hardest):

1. Your mom or dad is a money manager that pays meaningful commissions to the Street or is a key executive at a TSX-listed company. Most aspiring associates don't have this luxury.

2. You graduated from a top U.S. business school and interned at a U.S. bulge bracket firm. Doable but still not the common route.

Or most do it the hard way...

3. Get a job in a bank's corporate lending group doing credit analysis, or an accounting firm's valuation group, or any position where you can develop your financial modelling and analytical skills.

With few exceptions, candidates for research associate positions will have two to five years of work experience. Having one or more of the following experiences should help you get your first job as a research associate:

- **Summer internship.** Some of the larger investment firms offer summer internship programs

- **University co-op program.** A number of commerce programs allow students to gain practical work experience during their undergraduate years by alternating work and study terms

- **University investment programs.** Several universities (University of British Columbia, University of Calgary, University of New Brunswick, and Concordia University) offer a program where select commerce students, typically a group of eight, manage a portfolio of securities, participate in lectures by "mentors"

(Bay Street professionals), and are placed in summer positions with participating investment dealers and money management firms

## A Day in the Life of a Top Research Associate

**Mason Granger** is an associate analyst at RBC Capital Markets and part of the firm's income trust research team.

MBA from University of Toronto, 2002

Bachelor of Science (engineering chemistry) from Queen's University, 1996

I landed my first job on the Street as an equity research summer associate at a bulge bracket investment bank. For me, the summer internship was an invaluable experience and it gave me a foothold in the business and helped me get a full-time research associate position after graduating from the MBA program.

First-round interviews for the associate job can be difficult and often comprise a mix of questions that test the quantitative abilities of prospective associates, as well as the intentions and resolve to succeed in the role. Keeping in mind that a good analyst can distill the most complex problem into a solution that is defined by three simple points, candidates should be able to build a succinct and compelling response that offers just enough information to answer the question, and not a single detail more.

Through both personal experience and comparing notes with colleagues, it's safe to say that the greatest determinant of job satisfaction, as an associate, comes from the relationship with the senior analyst. It can be extremely rewarding to work with a senior analyst who is highly regarded by the

Street and has a track record of retaining associates and developing the next generation of talent.

As an associate, I have had the opportunity to meet some of the most influential leaders of corporate Canada and be on a first-name basis with some of the country's newsmakers. On the other hand, these glimpses of glory (and the promise of financial rewards at the analyst level) seem to ebb away at times when the reality of some of the more unpleasant aspects of the job set in. It is almost amusing, in a per-verse way, when I'm stuck at the office during earnings season. It's 11 p.m. and I'm seeing my freshly minted MBA put to good use as I dislodge the stubborn piece of paper that is jamming the photocopier!

Typically, I put in about 12 hours a day, and often more during earnings season. Here's what a typical day might look like:

**7:15 a.m.**    Arrive at work. Get coffee. Read *The Globe and Mail.* Quickly scan e-mail and various news services for break-ing industry and company news. Bring any material items to the analyst's attention.

**7:30 a.m.**    Attend the morning institutional meeting with the sales, trading, and research teams. As an associate, my partici-pation in these meetings is limited unless my analyst is out of town. Generally, I listen to what the other analysts have to say because news in other industry sectors may direct-ly or indirectly affect our companies.

**8:15 a.m.**    Back at my desk. Field a call from an institutional salesper-son regarding a piece of news on one of our companies. Pull together some data so that the salesperson can pass it along to a key institutional client before the market opens.

**8:45 a.m.**    Post a short message (regarding a question on relative valuation asked in the morning meeting) on an electronic bulletin board to be read by the salespeople and traders.

Clarification on a previously released news item on one of our companies comes across the news wire. Mildly positive; stock should open higher based on it.

**9:50 a.m.**  Grab a notebook and pen and head out the door to attend an annual general meeting (AGM) for one of our companies. At the end of the meeting, I corner the CFO to ask him how a new product rollout has been coming along. The company started shipping to key customers earlier than we had been anticipating. I may have to revisit the numbers in our model when I get back to the office.

**11:00 a.m.**  Back at the office. I update the models to incorporate information learned from the management presentation at the AGM. There is a slight upward revision to estimates based on the new guidance. Talk to my analyst and decide that the changes will warrant a quick note for the morning research package.

**12:00 p.m.**  Eat lunch at my desk. Scan industry websites for interesting tidbits on a number of key industries.

**12:30 p.m.**  My analyst announces that he has a 3 p.m. meeting with a major institutional client interested in several companies for which we've recently launched coverage. I'll need to update the analyst's presentation and comp table (comparative company analysis) as well.

**2:00 p.m.**  Hand off updated marketing package to my analyst for last-minute changes. Take the opportunity to check e-mail and return phone calls from institutional salespeople. Make changes to presentation suggested by my analyst and print copies for the meeting.

**2:30 p.m.**  Write up a quick research comment outlining estimate changes based on new information learned at this morning's AGM.

**4:00 p.m.**  Hand off draft morning comment to my analyst, who has just arrived back from his meeting. Call CFO of a new company that we're looking at in order to get clarification on accounting details and check some of our assumptions about her business. Make modest changes to financial model.

**6:00 p.m.**    Get handwritten changes to research comment from my analyst as he walks out the door. I'm briefly asked about the status of the launch of the coverage report and get a reminder that he'll want to see a draft in the morning. Call my wife and let her know that I hope to finish around 8 p.m.

**8:00 p.m.**    Shut down computer and take a few things off the printer to read when I get home.

## HOW RESEARCH ASSOCIATES SPEND THEIR TIME

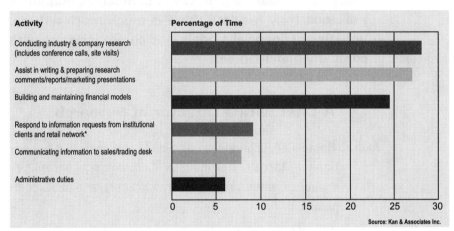

| Activity | Percentage of Time |
| --- | --- |
| Conducting industry & company research (includes conference calls, site visits) | |
| Assist in writing & preparing research comments/reports/marketing presentations | |
| Building and maintaining financial models | |
| Respond to information requests from institutional clients and retail network* | |
| Communicating information to sales/trading desk | |
| Administrative duties | |

Source: Kan & Associates Inc.

\* The retail network is typically serviced by a retail liason group – a team that acts as a "go-between" between the institutional equity research team and the retail brokers.

The above percentages tend to change depending on:

- **The length of the working relationship between the senior analyst and the associate.** Earlier on in an associate's relationship with the senior analyst, the analyst is not as likely to hand over a material portion of the report writing duties. These duties increase as the analyst gains trust in the associate's abilities.

- **The seniority/experience of the associate.** Experienced associates tend to get more responsibilities than less experienced ones.

- **The stage of the analyst's ramp-up mode.** As an analyst starts to roll out coverage of companies in his or her sector, the associate's time will be heavily skewed to building financial models, conducting company research, and assisting in the report writing. This situation can arise when a newly promoted analyst is initiating coverage or a seasoned analyst picks up coverage of another industry sector.

- **During earnings/reporting season (the period of time shortly after quarter-end when companies announce their quarterly results), there is much more writing, updating of financial models, and communicating with company management.**

## A Chat with a Director of Research

**Andrea Horan**, CFA, is partner and co-head of research at Genuity Capital Markets. Her industry coverage responsibilities include printers, publishers, broadcasters, and cable companies.

**Q. How did you get your start in the business?**

A. After graduating from the University of Toronto MBA program, I started working at Loewen, Ondaatje, McCutcheon as a research associate to three different analysts in three industry sectors. After about six months, one of my senior analysts left, so the firm offered me primary coverage responsibilities for the printing and publishing sectors.

**Q. Is it typical to see an associate take on analyst responsibilities after only six months on the job?**

A. No, but that's the great thing about working at an (institutional) boutique—you're likely going to be given more opportunities.

**Q. What lessons did you take away from your research associate experience?**

A. I learned that other associates in the firm are valuable resources, that the associate role throws you in the mix with a lot of competent professionals so one should take every opportunity to learn from them, and that accuracy in your work is critical.

**Q. Which of your other experiences in life best prepared you for your career as a sell-side analyst?**

A. The best preparation for being a sell-side analyst is being a sell-side analyst. One can only gain perspective by seeing the cycle tops and the cycle bottoms. There's a lot of insight that one gains over the years developing relationships (both with corporate management teams and institutional investors), marketing (learning to package the information as well as yourself), building credibility, and learning to effectively work as a team (with sales/trading/investment banking as well as with the associate).

**Q. So now as research boss, what qualities do you look for in a good research associate?**

A. I look for quick thinkers and candidates with strong financial acumen. In fact, I now make candidates take a short test. I may or may not give my associates a lot of quantitative work but I expect them to be able to catch any possible errors in our work, and that is only possible if they have a strong understanding of financial concepts.

**Q. How important is it that the candidates applying to your firm for an associate position have an interest in the stock market?**

A. I know that some senior people in a position to hire consider it important but I don't—I feel it's something that one can develop on the job.

Q. **What piece of advice would you want to pass on to people aspiring to start their careers in equity research (at the associate level)?**

A. I have several thoughts here: Once you've sent out your résumé, make it your full-time job to follow up. Don't get discouraged, because there's lots of turnover in this business so staffing needs change frequently. Don't get discouraged by a long interview process—it can take a long time to properly interview even a small pool of qualified candidates. Don't expect anyone in the business to spend a lot of time with you—but be appreciative when they do. Don't worry about salary in your first year—just get your foot in the door. Consider every job opportunity—don't simply hold out for the "perfect" job. Yes, working at a strong firm is better, and yes, working for a good analyst is better, but holding out may mean not ever getting a chance. "Good" firm or "bad," just get in there and make a name for yourself.

> "It's easier to switch teams than it is to get drafted."
> —*Bond Trader*

### Profile of the Ideal Associate Analyst Candidate

From a research director's perspective, the ideal associate analyst should meet the following criteria:

- strong financial modelling and quantitative skills
- good business writing skills
- a self-starter
- MBA or CA

- CFA or progress towards the designation
- prior industry-related work experience
- extremely detail-oriented
- a demonstrated passion for the investment business
- strong work ethic
- excellent communication skills (written and verbal)
- potential to be an analyst

### 12 Largest Fundamental
### Equity Research Teams in Canada*

| Company | Number of Team Members |
|---|---|
| 1. BMO Nesbitt Burns | 32 |
| 2. Scotia Capital | 27 |
| 3. TD Newcrest | 27 |
| 4. CIBC World Markets | 25 |
| 5. National Bank Financial | 25 |
| 6. RBC Capital Markets | 25 |
| 7. Desjardins Securities | 19 |
| 8. Canaccord Capital | 17 |
| 9. Sprott Securities | 17 |
| 10. Griffiths McBurney & Partners | 16 |
| 11. Dundee Securities | 14 |
| 12. Raymond James Canada | 14 |

*Measured by number of industry analysts based in Canada covering Canadian stocks.

## The Headhunter's View

### TIPS

1. **Know and understand the job you are applying for.** There's nothing worse than watching a candidate squirm and fumble their way through an interview trying to answer the simple question, What do you know about the position and the day-to-day responsibilities?

2. **Do some research on the company you're applying to.** Get a sense of who the *direct* competitors are and/or where the firm is on the food chain. For example, while most of the top 25 shops are, in a sense, competitors, the bank-owned dealers and the U.S. dealers directly compete against each other to the extent that they tend to play in the large-cap stocks and dominate the business in TSX 60 companies. These firms are considered tier one because both their reputational franchise and their business volumes (both trading and investment banking) tend to be consistently in the top 10 on the Street. Also, get a sense of the firm's (real or perceived) strengths and weaknesses either by function (equity trading/execution capabilities versus quality of equity research) or industry sector (a firm's health care franchise versus its mining franchise).

3. **Do some due diligence on the analyst you're applying to work for.** Your experience as an associate will depend largely on the analyst you work for. Compatibility with your analyst is probably the top consideration and a close second would be the amount of responsibility that he or she is willing to delegate to the associate. Also worth noting is the analyst's ranking in the independent analyst performance surveys.

4. **Do some due diligence on the firm's research director**. Find out what the research director's view is on upward mobility for research associates. Some firms have historically hired associates just for that role because they prefer to hire their senior analysts from industry—it's what gives their research a competitive edge. Other firms/research directors have a much more liberal view of promoting their young associates. If an associate has spent a couple of years of their working life making their senior analyst look good, they will get a shot at primary coverage responsibilities when an opportunity in the research department arises.

5. **Be able to talk intelligently about a company and its stock**. Research a company and be able to discuss the company's prospects. Be prepared to give three solid reasons why you would buy or short the company's stock.

6. **Better yet—write a research report and give it to potential employers**.

7. **Be able to name at least 10 brokerage firms in Canada**. That's a question that Michael Lam, a Managing Director at McFarlane Gordon, asks all potential young recruits. If you can't pass this simple test to show that you've done some homework on the industry, there's a high probability you're not coming back for round two of interviews. According to Lam, "Only a small percentage of recruits have ever been able to name 10 firms. I never gave a second interview to a person who couldn't name all ten."

8. **Consider the trade-off between working for a small firm versus working for a large (often bank-owned) dealer**. Smaller firms usually allow a more diverse career experience—more interaction with

professionals from other groups and better access to senior management. Furthermore, there tends to be less bureaucracy at smaller firms. Larger firms tend to offer a more structured environment but a brand name calling card.

9. **Don't ever underestimate the importance of interviews with the firm's other associates.** They can have almost as much veto power in the hiring process as the senior analyst.

"I was hired into this business (as a research associate) because my first boss was impressed that I had worked at McDonald's for years. In both jobs, you're simply standing in the trenches and doing the work. Sometimes you're sitting through dull meeting after dull meeting after dull meeting, just waiting to hear that one nugget of information that makes the difference. One of the things about our business that people don't fully appreciate is that everyone is very hard-working. And those that succeed are *incredibly* hard-working."

—*Duncan Stewart, CFA, Partner and*
*Portfolio Manager, Tera Capital*

## Suggested Reading

### Industry Analysis

1. *Entertainment Industry Economics: A Guide for Financial Analysis* (by Harold L. Vogel, published by Cambridge University Press)

A former top-ranked Wall Street leisure industry analyst shares his invaluable insights on understanding the economics of the entertainment industry. He provides coverage of a number of entertainment industries: movies, television, cable programming, broadcasting, publishing, music, casino gaming, sports, performing arts, theme parks, and toys.

2. *Fundamentals of Oil & Gas Accounting* (by Rebecca A. Gallun, et al., published by Pennwell Books)

Four professors with extensive backgrounds in both general accounting and petroleum accounting have put together this very comprehensive text.

3. *Handbook of Canadian Security Analysis, Volumes I & II* (edited by Joe Kan, published by John Wiley & Sons)

This valuable reference is a guide to evaluating the industry sectors of the market. Some 28 of Canada's top-ranked sell-side analysts were hand-picked to share their expertise and experience in understanding and analyzing the fundamental forces that drive stock performance in each industry group.

4. *Mining Explained: A Guide to Prospecting and Mining* (written and published by The Northern Miner)

The mining industry's source of information, *The Northern Miner*, has published this layman's guide to mining. This guide covers everything from basic geology to mining methods to mining company financials.

5. *Oil Company Financial Analysis in Nontechnical Language* (by Daniel Johnston, published by Pennwell Books)

The focus of this book is on the analysis of oil company assets, financial reports, and valuation of the related common stock. Although this book is targeted towards non-financial professionals, anyone looking to gain a better understanding of the oil & gas industry would be well-served by this text.

6. *Oil & Gas Pipeline Fundamentals* (by John L. Kennedy, published by Pennwell Books)

This book provides a good overview of the pipeline industry and pipeline operations.

7. *Travel Industry Economics: A Guide for Financial Analysis* (by Harold L. Vogel, published by Cambridge University Press)

Written by the same former star Wall Street analyst as *Entertainment Industry Economics*, this book focuses on the business economics of the various components of the travel industry.

### Fundamental Analysis

1. *Applied Equity Analysis: Stock Valuation Techniques for Wall Street Professionals* (by James English, published by McGraw-Hill)

Written by an equity analyst with twenty years of experience at JP Morgan, this book takes the reader through the entire valuation process from financial statement analysis through to the final investment recommendation.

2. *Cracking the Code: Financial Statements Explained* (by Ranjit Naik, published by Euromoney Books)

A guide for interpreting and analyzing financial statements.

3. *Damodaran on Valuation: Security Analysis for Investment and Corporate Finance* (by Aswath Damodaran, published by John Wiley & Sons)

An NYU Stern Business School finance professor provides a good overview of three valuation approaches for investment analysis: discounted cash flow, relative valuation, and contingent claim valuation.

4. *Equity Analysis, 2nd Edition* (by Eve Harvey, published by Euromoney Books)

This text examines the fundamental techniques used in valuing a company and its stock: financial statement analysis, ratio analysis, asset valuation, etc.

5. *Financial Modeling, 2nd Edition* (by Simon Benninga, published by MIT Press)

This is a good book on the fundamentals of spreadsheet modeling using Excel.

6. *Financial Statement Analysis: A Practitioner's Guide* (by Martin Fridson, published by John Wiley & Sons)

This is a practical guide for understanding and interpreting financial statements/reports. The author's use of real-world examples and conversational tone makes it an easier read than most finance texts.

7. *Fundamentals of Financial Analysis* (by Ranjit Naik, published by Euromoney Books)

This comprehensive text provides the reader with an understanding of the key concepts and techniques used in financial analysis.

8. *The Intelligent Investor* (by Benjamin Graham, published by Harper and Row)

   This classic text on value investing embodies the sound principles and investment philosophies that have produced other investment greats such as Warren Buffett.

9. *Security Analysis: Principles and Technique* (by Benjamin Graham and David L. Dodd, published by McGraw-Hill)

   Originally published in 1934, this book by Benjamin Graham and David Dodd continues to be regarded as a classic text on fundamental security analysis.

CHAPTER

2

# Sell-Side
# EQUITY ANALYST

# Sell-Side
# Equity Analyst

## Overview

THE SELL-SIDE EQUITY ANALYST (also known as *research analyst*) provides in-depth research and analysis on a single industry (or sometimes several related industries) and is therefore considered an expert in that specific industry sector. Unlike deal/transaction-oriented investment bankers, research analysts provide ongoing industry and company coverage. The institutional sales/trading desk looks to the analyst for timely insights on industry developments and company-specific investment ideas. The investment bankers look to the analyst for a more technical perspective (like a healthcare analyst may comment on the science behind a new vaccine) or simply the analyst's financial forecasts on the companies covered. Institutional and retail clients look to the analyst for industry knowledge, financial projections, and stock picks. The sell-side analyst is essentially the "go to" person within the brokerage firm for information on a particular industry and the companies within it.

Analysts often come up through the research department ranks after having served as research associates for two to four years. Associates that are deemed to have analyst potential and are ready to take on analyst responsibilities are given an opportunity when their senior analyst leaves the firm or when the firm is expanding research coverage in a certain industry sector. (At the time of writing, about half a dozen associates on the Street have just been promoted to analysts in the income trust sector.) However, not all firms promote associates to the analyst role. One energy boutique in Calgary, for example, only hires its analysts from industry. The firm's senior management feels it's the best way to differentiate the firm's research product from that of its competitors. Most firms, however, like to keep their associates motivated and hungry by dangling the carrot of future opportunities within the firm for those that excel.

Analysts also come from industry. Senior professionals from corporate Canada who are financially savvy, especially those from more technical industries like healthcare/biotech and mining, can bring a wealth of industry knowledge and industry contacts to the table.

> "First, learn the critical variables that define a company's success and focus on them. Second, figure out how to be different. Being a top analyst means more than just being a good thinker. Your research and efforts have to show well in order to grab the mindshare of busy portfolio managers."
> —*Dana Benner, Equity Research, Westwind Partners*

### Education

When hiring analysts for most industry sectors, the primary consideration is relevant work experience, and educational background is secondary. However, there are a couple of industry sectors where candidates should have a more technical academic background. More often than not, sell-side analysts in the healthcare/biotech sector have some kind of health sciences undergraduate and/or masters degree (bio-chemistry, pharmacology, etc.), and analysts in the junior mining space have an earth sciences background (geology, mineral exploration, etc.). Candidates without these backgrounds have been hired as analysts in those sectors, but with mixed results. When a mining exploration company's prospects are based on the results of one drill hole or an emerging biotech company's prospects are based on evaluating early Phase II clinical trials, an analyst needs to have the technical background to have credibility. A glance at the top five ranked analysts in the biotech/pharmaceuticals sector confirms the point—all five have health sciences backgrounds.

### Compensation Range

At the tier one firms, the average total annual compensation for an analyst is in the range of $500,000 to $550,000. Junior analysts and senior (non-star) analysts are paid less, whereas a firm's A-team analysts are paid north of $700,000.

At the tier two firms, the average compensation for an analyst is in the range of $250,000 to $400,000.

#### Regulatory Issues Affecting Analyst Compensation

In April 2003, 10 of Wall Street's biggest brokerages paid a collective fine of $1.4 billion to settle charges of conflict of interest between research and investment banking. The global settlement struck with the U.S. Securities and Exchange Commission and New York State Attorney General Eliot Spitzer outlined a number of key reforms for the securities industry. Front and center of the reforms were efforts to sever ties between equity research and investment banking. More specifically, there is to be no direct or indirect link between analyst compensation and investment banking revenues. In fact, I-bankers are not to have any influence on analyst compensation. And in an effort to make analysts accountable for their stock recommendations, analyst compensation should also factor in the performance of stock calls.

In Canada, the Investment Dealers Association has issued Policy 11—Research Restrictions and Disclosure Requirements to address sell-side analyst conflicts of interest. Policy 11 is largely based on the Securities Industry Committee on Analyst Standards' *Crawford Report* published in October 2001. (See Appendix 1—Policy 11.)

Exhibit 1 is an analyst compensation plan from a global dealer that no longer has an institutional equity team in Canada. This plan (or "scorecard" as it was called by former research staffers at the firm) was effective pre-Spitzer and was representative of most of the dealers in that it explicitly tied investment banking revenues to analyst compensation. Furthermore, there is seemingly no financial incentive to make the right stock picks.

### Exhibit 1—Pre-Spitzer Analyst Compensation Plan

| Measure | Target |
| --- | --- |
| *Wealth Management* | |
| Number of private client presentations | 2 |
| *Corporate Finance and Advisory Division* | |
| Number of corporate finance ideas that are executed | 4 |
| *Research/Product Marketing* | |
| Percent of target accounts ranking analyst in the top three | 75% |
| Percent of market share trading in covered companies | 15% |
| Number of companies covered | 8 |
| Number of Company Reports per covered company | 2 |
| Number of Morning Comments per month | 12 |
| Number of Research Notes per month | 8 |
| Number of Thematic Sector/Industry pieces produced per annum (participation in global pieces) | 2 |
| Number of road shows per annum (requested by account managers) | 2 |

| | |
|---|---|
| Number of one-on-ones per annum | 250 |
| Number of calls per week (to target accounts) | 20–25 |
| Number of hosted company luncheons/one-on-one series per annum | 3 |

*Peer Review*
| | |
|---|---|
| Rating by peers | High |

Exhibit 2 is a typical analyst compensation plan from the domestic bank-owned investment dealers in Canada. This plan, drafted post-Spitzer, does not *explicitly* tie analyst compensation to investment banking revenues. It does, however, factor in an analyst's performance in making good stock calls.

### Exhibit 2—Post-Spitzer Analyst Compensation Plan

The factors that affect analysts' compensation:

• the analyst's performance in picking stocks

• votes from institutional investors in the firm's top accounts

• results achieved in surveys of institutional investors

• peer reviews

• retail trading commissions in the analyst's sector and feedback from the retail system

• institutional trading commissions in the analyst's sector and feedback from the firm's institutional traders

• the analyst's contribution to the firm's corporate marketing program of getting company managements in front of institutional investors

• overall productivity

• compensation levels at competitor firms

## Industry Certification

CFA Institute administers the CFA program. The program covers topics such as corporate finance, economics, portfolio management, and financial statement analysis.

To earn the CFA charter, a CFA candidate must pass three six-hour examinations (CFA Institute suggests that 250 hours of study is needed to prepare for each exam) and have spent three years working in a role where he or she is involved in the investment decision-making process.

The failure rate for each of the exams tends to hover around 50%. Of the approximately 56,000 CFA charterholders, few have passed all three exams consecutively.

The CFA designation has become the standard in the investment/finance industry. The program may or may not make you a better stock picker, but successful completion of the program has become a rite of passage into the institutional investment community. Most research directors prefer to see candidates who have obtained the designation or are making progress towards completing the program.

## A Day in the Life of a Top Sell-Side Analyst

**Ben Cherniavsky** is a research analyst at Raymond James Canada. In the 2004 BWI Institutional Equity Performance Report, he was the #1 ranked small cap/special situations analyst in Canada. Mr. Cherniavsky was also named as one of the top five Canadian stock pickers in 2003 by the StarMine/Financial Post Survey.

MBA from University of Western Ontario, 1998

Bachelor of Arts (economics and political science) from University of Alberta, 1994

My move to an analyst position came through very conventional means. After graduating from my MBA program, I took a job as a research associate with

Goepel Shields and Partners, the predecessor firm to Raymond James Ltd. My initial role was to assist the research director with his coverage of "special situations" stocks. At the time, for Goepel this broadly included any company that was non-resource related.

Although the pay with Goepel was well below that which many of my classmates had negotiated with bulge bracket dealers, I viewed this as an excellent opportunity for three reasons. First, the research director was very experienced and a well-respected analyst on the Street. Second, I was attracted to the entrepreneurial culture of an employee-owned firm and the potential financial upside to any equity that I was able to attain over time. Finally, and perhaps most importantly, the firm was growing rapidly and looking to expand its research coverage universe beyond its traditional niche of mining, energy, and forestry. This meant that new analyst opportunities would likely transpire much faster at Goepel than at a more mature bank-owned dealer.

Fortunately, everything went according to plan. After six months of proving myself in the research department, I was offered the opportunity to develop my own analyst franchise in the industrial products & services sector. Then, within another 18 months, Raymond James, a mid-market U.S. investment dealer, purchased Goepel and I now work for a firm that has a very unique North American equity markets strategy.

As for the day-to-day routine of an analyst, it is arguably one of the most exciting desk jobs imaginable. In addition to waking up every morning not knowing what to expect from the market, you are provided with daily direct access to some of the best CEOs in the country and an endless list of the most sophisticated and influential investors around. This privilege, however, comes with considerable demands. Whether you are tuned into a conference call or combing through the footnotes of a company's latest quarterly results, an analyst's day is never really done. Even during times when news flow in your sector tends to ebb, there are always client calls to make and industry data to read. In fact, it is often these days of relative calm that prove to be most valuable insofar as they facilitate opportunities to thoroughly analyze your companies, come up with creative investment themes, undertake investigative research, develop robust financial models, and publish quality reports. Ultimately, gaining an edge in these areas is what most often separates the great analysts from the rest of the pack.

Then there is the travel. A strong analyst in a hot sector can spend up to half his time on the road. Investment research is, after all, a people business. And for the sell-side analyst, the candle burns at both ends. On one hand, the job requires him or her to spend countless hours presenting to portfolio managers in all corners of the continent. This is really the only way to get your research ideas heard, understood, and paid for. On the other hand, developing solid insight into a company most effectively comes from spending quality time with its management team, talking to its customers, and visiting its operations, wherever they may be in the world. The glamour associated with this kind of continuous travel wears off pretty quickly. Nevertheless, it is a unique and stimulating experience that is not commonly found in other professions.

Of course, there is the potential for sizable rewards from this gruelling analyst schedule. Not only can the financial upside be exceedingly large, but there is also the opportunity for intrinsic job satisfaction. It may sound strange, but there is a real adrenaline rush when your out-of-consensus call on a stock proves to be right. Indeed, doing this repeatedly—with marked skill and a little bit of luck—can earn an analyst all-star status. Modest amounts of glory and fortune usually follow.

Bear in mind that I am in the unusual position of working as a sell-side analyst in Vancouver and am therefore three hours behind the normal operating hours of North America's major markets. While there are some advantages to this, the biggest downside is the early mornings. A typical day in the office for me starts at 4:30 a.m. local time and may transpire as follows:

**4:30 a.m.** From home, dial into the U.S. morning conference call for the sales and trading desk. I contribute a few comments about my new report on why the stock of company X is set to soar in the next 12 months.

**5:00 a.m.** Dial into the morning conference call for the Canadian sales and trading desk. Repeat remarks made in U.S. call on company X. Respond to a few questions from salespeople.

**5:30 a.m.** Get ready for work; have breakfast while perusing overnight e-mails, newspaper headlines, and industry developments.

**6:30 a.m.** Arrive at the office. I check opening quotes for all companies covered, and notice that stock of company X is up 5%, perhaps in response to the publication of our bullish report.

**6:45 a.m.** Phone rings from client in Montreal. She wants to discuss the assumptions used in our valuation section of the company X report. Generally, she agrees with our conclusions and indicates that the fund would be inclined to buy the stock on weakness.

**7:15 a.m.** Get off the phone with Montreal client; call trading desk to inform them of the potential buyer. Then I check the two voicemails that were left for me while I was on the phone. One is from the sales desk regarding the company X report; the other is from a Toronto client looking for a copy of our financial model for company Y. Return calls.

**8:00 a.m.**    Stock for company Z gets halted. Management issues press release of major acquisition. The sales desk immediately calls to discuss my initial reaction. I offer some limited comments.

**8:10 a.m.**    Discuss implications of the transaction with associate. Call company Z management to get more information, then ask associate to input new variables into our model. I return three clients' phone calls that piled up over the past 10 minutes, and share my impressions with them of what the news means for the stock.

**9:00 a.m.**    Carefully check and analyze the conclusions that my associate has made in our model for company Z. We discuss what we should do with our rating. We decide that an upgrade is justified and I ask my associate to begin writing a report.

**10:00 a.m.**    Attend scheduled meeting with CEO of company V at their head office across the street. I ask for an update on the business outlook, discuss the source of margin erosion in the last quarter, etc. I request an invitation to inspect the operations of their recently acquired assets in South America sometime in the next six weeks.

**11:30 a.m.**    Return to the office. I get an update from associate on status of report, and check my voicemails and e-mails. A salesperson comes to collect me for a lunch booked with a local portfolio manager.

**12:00 p.m.**    Have lunch with this local client at a downtown restaurant. We discuss the company X report, company Z announcement, and information gathered while meeting with CEO of company V earlier that morning.

**2:00 p.m.**   Back at the office. I check closing prices, and place a few calls to key clients interested in hearing what the CEO of company V told me.

**3:00 p.m.**   Day begins to slow down. My attention is turned to our pending research report on the rising level of competition in the heavy equipment industry. Read annual reports of U.S. competitors to the Canadian companies in our coverage universe. I browse the Web for information on market trends, and call customers in the aerospace industry.

**5:00 p.m.**   Review and approve associate's report on company Z acquisition. Prepare a blast voicemail message for clients and some short comments for tomorrow morning's calls.

**5:30 p.m.**   Shut down computer and go home to pack bags for tomorrow's marketing trip to the U.S. west coast.

## HOW SELL-SIDE ANALYSTS SPEND THEIR TIME

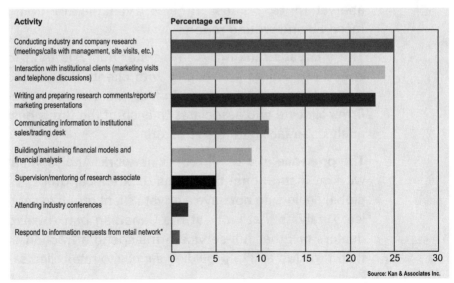

* The retail network is typically serviced by a retail liason group – a team that acts as a "go-between" between the institutional equity research team and the retail brokers.

The above percentages tend to change depending on:

- **The stage of the analyst's "life cycle"**. A new analyst (or an experienced analyst that has just switched firms) will spend a higher-than-average amount of time conducting company/industry research, building the financial models, and writing/preparing research reports, and a lower-than-average amount of time interacting with institutional investors. Once he or she has built up a critical mass of research (typically six to eight companies under coverage), the time allocation is reversed such that a higher-than-average amount of time is spent interacting with/marketing to institutional clients.

- **Geographic location of the analyst**. Analysts based outside of Toronto tend to have a higher proportion of marketing-related travel, given that the majority of institutional investors are based in Toronto.

- **The market sentiment towards the industry sector**. In a hot market, the sales desk will want to market the analyst more, so less time is available for doing research and writing reports.

- **The analyst's ranking**. A firm's star analysts tend to spend more time interacting with clients than doing research or writing reports. In fact, most of the larger firms allocate two associates to each of the firm's best analysts to facilitate this structure.

- **The presence of a retail broker network**. Analysts that work at institutional boutiques or the local offices of global dealers do not have a private client group to service. Analysts that work at the Canadian bank-owned dealers or other full-service firms spend a fraction of their time (up to 3%) providing service to retail clients.

## A Chat with a Research Director

**Steve Garmaise** has been a research director for the past 10 years and a sell-side analyst for the previous 12 years. He was most recently the global head of equity research at RBC Capital Markets. Prior to that, he was both the director of Canadian research and deputy director of North American research at Merrill Lynch Canada. His first stint of managing a research department was at First Marathon Securities.

**Q. How did you get your start in the business?**

A. My first job on the Street was as an investment analyst at Confederation Life. Back then, the standard entry-level investment analyst job was within the investment team at one of the large life insurance companies. My unusual background (i.e., no undergraduate degree and seven years in a kibbutz in Israel before doing my MBA at University of Western Ontario) made the job search after UWO rather difficult. However, my internship at Gardner Watson (a small sell-side boutique) during the previous summer helped me land a spot at Confederation Life. Interestingly enough, they were reluctant to hire me at first because they thought that I would use the position as a stepping stone to the "brighter lights and better pay" of the sell-side.

**Q. But they still hired you?**

A. Yes, and after a year, I left for the "brighter lights and better pay" of the sell-side. I joined Wood Gundy as a special situations analyst.

**Q. What did you like most about the sell-side analyst experience?**

A. The three things that I loved most about the job were:

a. Being paid to learn. Every day was different and every day had its own set of challenges, but it was a great learning experience.

b. Being encouraged to be different. One is rewarded for having creative insights into what makes a company tick and what factors change the Street's perception of a company and its value in the marketplace.

c. Dealing with some of the smartest people around. The investment business tends to attract the best and the brightest, and some of the most competitive people out there. And I thoroughly enjoyed the daily competition with my peers.

And I also enjoy telling a good story—every successful analyst knows how to tell a good story.

**Q. Did you ever consider moving over to the sales desk?**

A. I prefer to know a lot about a little as opposed to a little about a lot. I like to dig deeper on stories and as a salesperson, you don't have the time or luxury to do that. And I think many analysts deep down enjoy being the centre of attention and being quoted in the press and you don't get that same profile as a salesperson.

**Q. Having been a research director at several platforms (i.e., a successful independent boutique, the Canadian office of a U.S. bulge-bracket dealer, and then a domestic bank-owned dealer), how is the analyst function different at the various platforms?**

A.   At the margin, there are some small differences in terms of the overall research product delivered. For example, research at the domestic bank-owned dealers has a higher maintenance component to it. The big retail investor base also requires broader coverage, in terms of both industries covered and companies covered within each industry. However, the fundamental job of an analyst remains the same regardless of the platform: getting the best information and deriving the most insightful analysis such that institutional clients continuously use, and pay for, the research.

**Q.   In what ways has the new regulatory environment changed the day-to-day life of an analyst?**

A.   I can speak to my experience at the bank-owned dealer as Policy 11 was being adopted by the Street and there were, and continue to be, more regulatory hassles: An analyst now has to log every conversation with the press—that's not an effective use of an analyst's time. Every recommendation change has to be pre-approved by research management— another layer of bureaucracy. Personal trading in any of the stocks in an analyst's own industry is banned because of the potential for a conflict of interest, whereas some still believe that an analyst should be able to put their money where their mouth is and invest in the stocks they cover. The industry has now become obsessed with avoiding even the *appearance* of being in a potential conflict of interest.

**Q.   There's been some controversy as to the longer-term trend of analyst compensation. Any comments?**

A.   The credibility, and therefore the value, of research was challenged after the tech bubble. The industry has since taken a number of measures to regain investor confidence and it'll be interesting to see how it all evolves. The analyst job will remain lucrative but it won't pay the way it used to.

**Q. What quality do you look for when hiring for the analyst role?**

A. I look for people who know their own strengths and weaknesses and know how to differentiate themselves based on their strengths. Above a certain minimum level of quantitative ability, analysts can define their own franchise by playing to their own strengths. A CA-type can gain a competitive edge by having the best models and perhaps the most accurate earnings estimates, or an analyst can have excellent industry sources and therefore be tuned in to the industry scuttlebutt. I want to know that the analyst can provide value-added to the client community.

"Money managers, especially those who have been in the business for a few market cycles, look for analysts with a fresh approach and a unique angle."

*—Former top-ranked senior analyst*

### Profile of the Ideal Sell-Side Analyst Candidate

From a research director's perspective, the ideal sell-side analyst should meet the following criteria:

- strong financial modelling and quantitative skills
- prior industry-related work experience
- excellent client interaction skills
- a self-starter
- MBA or CA
- CFA or progress towards the designation
- strong work ethic
- excellent communication skills (written and verbal)
- detail-oriented

## Comparing a Sell-Side Analyst
## with a Buy-Side Analyst

|  | Sell-side Analyst | Senior Buy-side Analyst |
|---|---|---|
| Starting total compensation | $100,000 | $100,000 |
| Range of total compensation | $100,000 to $1 million+ | $100,000 to $500,000 |
| Percentage of comp for stock picking | Minority | Majority |
| Number of industries covered | Typically one | Typically two to four |
| Number of companies covered | 10–15 | 30–50 |
| Goal of research | To generate investment ideas that make clients money and therefore generate trading commissions | To generate investment ideas for fund/investment performance |
| User of research | Internal clients: sales/trading team<br><br>External clients: institutional and retail | Internal client: portfolio manager(s) |
| Work hours | 60-hour-plus workweeks | 50-hour workweeks |
| Common career paths | Buy-side, corporate role, I-sales | Portfolio manager |
| Upside in bull markets | Potential for *significant* increase in comp | Potential for *incremental* increase in comp |
| Downside in bear markets | Higher risk of general headcount reductions | Lower risk of layoffs |

## Life After Being a Sell-Side Analyst

After having acquired and mastered the primary skills of the job (doing thorough fundamental research on companies; understanding the economic, competitive, and internal drivers of a company's earnings and its stock price; and understanding the capital markets process), a sell-side analyst has several attractive career options to move on to.

- **Buy-side.** Experience as an analyst on the sell-side lends itself well to making a switch to the buy-side as an analyst or money manager. Typically, analysts from the sell-side move to the buy-side as senior analysts. A few of the most seasoned and best-ranked sell-siders make the move directly into a portfolio manager role.

- **Research director.** While some of the administrative aspects of this role can make it a thankless job, the idea of being top dog still makes this a coveted position by many. At the independent firms and the Canadian offices of the global dealers, the director of research tends to take on the role of player/coach (i.e., the head of research will wear two hats—that of an analyst/producer as well as that of manager). At the larger bank-owned securities dealers, however, the research director's only job is to run the department. In fact, there is usually a deputy/assistant research director as well. The responsibility of reading the volume of research (morning notes, industry reports, company reports, etc.) produced by the department's thirty or so analysts on 300 to 400 companies is very time-consuming. Not to mention the time spent managing the department's relationship with the retail network, or the time spent hiring and firing.

- **Corporate role (IR, corporate development, business development).** Having acquired an intimate knowledge of a company (and its competitors and the industry) and built relationships with the key executives, a senior role on the corporate side is an attractive option for those that want to take the intensity level down a notch.

- **Investment banking.** The relationships that a sell-side analyst has with the key executives at the corporate issuers would serve him or her well as an investment banker.

- **Institutional sales.** The established relationships with the institutional money managers makes an analyst valuable to the firm, while the strong analytical abilities and intimate knowledge of the companies makes the analyst value-added to the institutional accounts by virtue of the fact that he or she can talk the talk with the buy-side analysts and portfolio managers.

### The 12 Largest Fundamental Equity Research Teams in Canada*

| Company | Number of Team Members |
|---|---|
| 1. BMO Nesbitt Burns | 32 |
| 2. Scotia Capital | 27 |
| 3. TD Newcrest | 27 |
| 4. CIBC World Markets | 25 |
| 5. National Bank Financial | 25 |
| 6. RBC Capital Markets | 25 |
| 7. Canaccord Capital | 17 |
| 8. Sprott Securities | 17 |
| 9. Desjardins Securities | 17 |
| 10. Griffiths McBurney & Partners | 16 |
| 11. Dundee Securities | 14 |
| 12. Raymond James Canada | 14 |

*Measured by number of industry analysts based in Canada covering Canadian stocks.

## Analyst Performance Surveys

There are four surveys in North America that provide annual rankings of Canadian sell-side analysts:

1. StarMine/*Financial Post* Survey: Canada's Best Analysts

2. *The Wall Street Journal's* "Best on the Street"

3. Greenwich Associates Stock Brokerage Programs

4. Brendan Wood International Survey – Institutional Equity Research, Sales and Trading Performance in Canada

The first two attempt to provide more quantitative measures of analyst performance by collecting and analyzing data relating to analysts' stock recommendations and earnings estimates over the course of the year. The latter two are more qualitative in that they survey the buy-side of the Street for their opinions/comments on sell-side analysts.

Brokerage firms buy these surveys to:

a. simply get a better understanding of how they are perceived/regarded by the institutional clients

b. use the information/results as additional inputs in determining analyst compensation

c. use the (favourable) ranking results in marketing pitches to corporate clients

### 1. StarMine/*Financial Post* Survey: Canada's Best Analysts

San Francisco-based StarMine collects data on every North American analyst estimate, revision, and recommendation recorded by the Thomson First Call and I/B/E/S databases. The StarMine Survey then evaluates analysts on how well they serve investors based on two criteria: stock-picking performance and accuracy of earnings estimates. Stock-picking prowess is measured by calculating both an "absolute return" and an "excess return" (a relative return measure that isolates the skill of the analyst in picking the best-performing stocks in his or her coverage universe independent of the direction of the broader market). The results of the Canadian analysts are published in the *Financial Post* in April and the results of the U.S. analysts are released on Forbes.com in May.

## 2. *The Wall Street Journal's* "Best on the Street"

The "Best on the Street" Survey (a joint effort between *The Wall Street Journal* and Thomson Financial) tries to identify the top five stock pickers in each of 49 industries. Analysts are ranked on the performance of their stock recommendations for the previous year (based on data collected and calculated by Thomson First Call throughout the year). The results are published in a special section each May.

Although the WSJ Survey is U.S.-centric, it is included in this discussion because Canadian analysts manage to capture a few spots in the rankings most years. In 2002, for example, there were 36 eligible analysts in the mining & metals category; the top five all were Canadian-based analysts.

## 3. Greenwich Associates Stock Brokerage Programs

The Greenwich survey ranks analysts by institutional client feedback. One of the distinguishing characteristics of this survey is that, because of the short questionnaires, they manage to solicit a high number of respondents at the more senior levels. The report is released in April of each year.

Analysts are evaluated on the following: knowledge of industry fundamentals, written research reports, creative investment ideas, and level of service.

**4. Brendan Wood International Survey: Institutional Equity Research, Sales and Trading Performance in Canada**

The BWI survey, the more established of the two qualitative surveys, ranks analysts based on the survey results of institutional investors. It is published in June of each year.

Analysts are evaluated on the following: perceived quality of research coverage, accounts that report paying for the analyst, percent of relationships in the BWI panel, average share of commissions, quality of investment ideas, knowledge of the sector, level of contact, quality of written reports, credibility of analyst's research, and BWI momentum factor.

## Suggested Reading

### Industry Analysis

1. *Entertainment Industry Economics: A Guide for Financial Analysis* (by Harold L. Vogel, published by Cambridge University Press)

A former top-ranked Wall Street leisure industry analyst shares his invaluable insights on understanding the economics of the entertainment industry. He provides coverage of a number of entertainment industries: movies, television, cable programming, broadcasting, publishing, music, casino gaming, sports, performing arts, theme parks, and toys.

2. *Fundamentals of Oil & Gas Accounting* (by Rebecca A. Gallun, et al., published by Pennwell Books)

   Four professors with extensive backgrounds in both general accounting and petroleum accounting have put together this very comprehensive text.

3. *Handbook of Canadian Security Analysis, Volumes I & II* (edited by Joe Kan, published by John Wiley & Sons)

   This valuable reference is a guide to evaluating the industry sectors of the market. Some 28 of Canada's top-ranked sell-side analysts were hand-picked to share their expertise and experience in understanding and analyzing the fundamental forces that drive stock performance in each industry group.

4. *Mining Explained: A Guide to Prospecting and Mining* (written and published by The Northern Miner)

   The mining industry's source of information, *The Northern Miner*, has published this layman's guide to mining. This guide covers everything from basic geology to mining methods to mining company financials.

5. *Oil Company Financial Analysis in Nontechnical Language* (by Daniel Johnston, published by Pennwell Books)

   The focus of this book is on the analysis of oil company assets, financial reports, and valuation of the related common stock. Although this book is targeted towards non-financial professionals, anyone looking to gain a better understanding of the oil & gas industry would be well-served by this text.

6. *Oil & Gas Pipeline Fundamentals* (by John L. Kennedy, published by Pennwell Books)

This book provides a good overview of the pipeline industry and pipeline operations.

7. *Travel Industry Economics: A Guide for Financial Analysis* (by Harold L. Vogel, published by Cambridge University Press)

Written by the same former star Wall Street analyst as *Entertainment Industry Economics*, this book focuses on the business economics of the various components of the travel industry.

### Fundamental Analysis

1. *Applied Equity Analysis: Stock Valuation Techniques for Wall Street Professionals* (by James English, published by McGraw-Hill)

Written by an equity analyst with 20 years of experience at JP Morgan, this book takes the reader through the entire valuation process, from financial statement analysis through to the final investment recommendation.

2. *Cracking the Code: Financial Statements Explained* (by Ranjit Naik, published by Euromoney Books)

A guide for interpreting and analyzing financial statements.

3. *Damodaran on Valuation: Security Analysis for Investment and Corporate Finance* (by Aswath Damodaran, published by John Wiley & Sons)

An NYU Stern Business School finance professor provides a good overview of three valuation approaches for investment analysis: discounted cash flow, relative valuation, and contingent claim valuation.

4. *Equity Analysis, 2nd Edition* (by Eve Harvey, published by Euromoney Books)

   A detailed treatment of the principles behind equity analysis.

5. *Financial Modeling, 2nd Edition* (by Simon Benninga, published by MIT Press)

   This is a good book on the fundamentals of spreadsheet modeling using Excel.

6. *Financial Statement Analysis: A Practitioner's Guide* (by Martin Fridson and Fernando Alvarez, published by John Wiley & Sons)

   This is a practical guide for understanding and interpreting financial statements and reports. The author's use of real-world examples and conversational tone makes it an easier read than most finance texts.

7. *Fundamentals of Financial Analysis* (by Ranjit Naik, published by Euromoney Books)

   This comprehensive text provides the reader with an understanding of the key concepts and techniques used in financial analysis.

8. *The Intelligent Investor* (by Benjamin Graham, published by Harper and Row)

This classic text on value investing embodies the sound principles and investment philosophies that have produced other investment greats such as Warren Buffett.

9. *Security Analysis: Principles and Technique* (by Benjamin Graham and David L. Dodd, published by McGraw-Hill)

   Originally published in 1934, this book continues to be regarded as a classic text on fundamental security analysis.

"With respect to the current and future challenges in our industry, the overriding theme is trust and the need to rebuild trust and confidence amongst all constituents. While the governance experts can articulate best practices and the regulators can prescribe new rules, I contend that trust, which is earned, begins at home with one's personal integrity and one's ability to distinguish between right and wrong."

—*Rod Sim, Former CEO, Orion Securities*

# APPENDIX

## Policy No. 11
### Research Restrictions and Disclosure Requirements

## Introduction

This Policy establishes requirements that analysts must follow when publishing research reports or making recommendations. These requirements represent the minimum procedural requirements that Members must have in place to minimize potential conflicts of interest. The Disclosure required under Policy No. 11 must be clear, comprehensive and prominent. Boilerplate disclosure is not sufficient.

These requirements are based on the recommendations of the Securities Industry Committee on Analyst Standards with input from both industry and non-industry groups.

## Definitions

"advisory capacity" means providing advice to an issuer in return for remuneration, other than advice with respect to trading and related services.

"analyst" means any partner, director, officer, employee or agent of a Member who is held out to the public as an analyst or whose responsibilities to the Member include the preparation of any written report for distribution to clients or prospective clients of the Member which includes a recommendation with respect to a security.

"equity related security" means a security whose performance is based on the performance of an underlying equity security or a basket of income producing assets. Securities classified as an equity related security include, without limitation, convertible securities and income trust units.

"investment banking service" includes, without limitation, acting as an underwriter in an offering for the issuer; acting as a financial adviser in a merger or acquisition; providing venture capital, lines of credit, or serving as a placement agent for the issuer.

"research report" means any written or electronic communication that the Member has distributed or will distribute to its clients or the general public, which contains an analyst's recommendation concerning the purchase, sale or holding of a security (but shall exclude all government debt and government guaranteed debt).

"remuneration" means any good, service or other benefit, monetary or otherwise, that could be provided to or received by an analyst.

"supervisory analyst" means an officer of the Member designated as being responsible for research.

## Requirements

1. Each Member shall have written conflict of interest policies and procedures, in order to minimize conflicts faced by analysts. All such policies must be approved by and filed with the Association.

2. Each Member shall prominently disclose in any research report:

   (a) any information regarding its, or its analyst's business with or relationship with any issuer which is the subject of the report which might reasonably be expected to indicate a potential conflict of interest on the part of the Member or the analyst in making a recommendation with regard to the issuer. Such information includes, but is not limited to:

      (i) whether, as of the end of the month immediately preceding the date of issuance of the research report or the end of the second most recent month if the issue date is less than 10 calendar days after the end of the most recent month, the Member and its affiliates collectively beneficially own 1% or more of any class of the issuer's equity securities,

(ii) whether the analyst or any associate of the analyst responsible for the report or recommendation or any individuals directly involved in the preparation of the report hold or are short any of the issuer's securities directly or through derivatives,

(iii) whether any partner, director or officer of a Member or any analyst involved in the preparation of a report on the issuer has, during the preceding 12 months provided services to the issuer for remuneration other than normal course investment advisory or trade execution services,

(iv) whether the Member firm has provided investment banking services for the issuer during the 12 months preceding the date of issuance of the research report or recommendation,

(v) the name of any partner, director, officer, employee or agent of the Member who is an officer, director or employee of the issuer, or who serves in any advisory capacity of the issuer, and

(vi) whether the Member is making a market in an equity or equity related security of the subject issue.

(b) the Member's system for rating investment opportunities and how each recommendation fits within the system and shall disclose on their websites or otherwise, quarterly, the percentage of its recommendations that fall into each category of their recommended terminology; and

(c) its policies and procedures regarding the dissemination of research.

A Member shall comply with subsections (b) and (c) by disclosing such information in the report or by disclosing in the report where such information can be obtained.

3. Where an employee of a Member makes a public comment (which shall include an interview) about the merits of an issuer or its securities, a reference must be made to the existence of any relevant research report issued by the Member containing the disclosure as required above, if one exists, or it must be disclosed that such a report does not exist.

4. Where a Member distributes a research report prepared by an independent third party to its clients under the third party name, the Member must disclose any items which would be required to be disclosed under requirement 2 of Policy No. 11 had the report been issued in the Member's name. This requirement does not apply to research reports issued by Members of the National Association of Securities Dealers ("NASD") or issued by persons governed by other regulators approved by the Investment Dealers Association, and does not apply if the Member simply provides to clients access to the independent third party research reports or provides independent third party research at the request of clients. However, where this requirement does not apply, Members must disclose that such research is not prepared subject to Canadian disclosure requirements.

5. No Member shall issue a research report prepared by an analyst if the analyst or any associate of the analyst serves as an officer, director or employee of the issuer or serves in any advisory capacity to the issuer.

6. Any Member that distributes research reports to clients or prospective clients in its own name must disclose its

research dissemination policies and procedures on its website or by other means.

7. Each Member who distributes research reports to clients or prospective clients shall have policies and procedures reasonably designed to prohibit any trading by its partners, directors, officers, employees or agents resulting in an increase, a decrease, or liquidation of a position in a listed security, or a derivative instrument based principally on a listed or quoted security, with knowledge of or in anticipation of the distribution of a research report, a new recommendation or a change in a recommendation relating to a security that could reasonably be expected to have an effect on the price of the security.

8. No individual directly involved in the preparation of the report can effect a trade in a security of an issuer, or a derivative instrument whose value depends principally on the value of a security of an issuer, regarding which the analyst has an outstanding recommendation for a period of 30 calendar days before and 5 calendar days after issuance of the research report, unless that individual receives the previous written approval of a designated partner, officer or director of the Member. No approval may be given to allow an analyst or any individual involved in the preparation of the report to make a trade that is contrary to the analyst's current recommendation, unless special circumstances exist.

9. Members must disclose in research reports if in the previous 12 months the analyst responsible for preparing the report received compensation based upon the Member's investment banking revenues.

10. No Member may pay any bonus, salary or other form of compensation to an analyst that is directly based upon one or more specific investment banking services transactions.

11. Each Member shall have policies and procedures in place reasonably to prevent recommendations in research reports from being influenced by the investment-banking department or the issuer. Such policies and procedures shall, at minimum:

   (i) prohibit any requirement for approval of research reports by the investment banking department;

   (ii) limit comments from the investment banking department on research reports to correction of factual errors;

   (iii) prevent the investment banking department from receiving advance notice of ratings or rating changes on covered companies; and

   (iv) establish systems to control and keep records of the flow of information between analysts and investment banking departments regarding issuers that are the subject of current or prospective research reports.

12. No Member may directly or indirectly offer favourable research, a specific rating or a specific price target, a delay in changing a rating or price target or threaten to change research, a rating or a price target of an issuer as consideration or inducement for the receipt of business or compensation from an issuer.

13. Members must disclose in research reports if and to what extent an analyst has viewed the material operations of an issuer. Members must also disclose where there has been a payment or reimbursement by the issuer of the analyst's travel expenses for such visit.

14. No Member may issue a research report for an equity or equity related security regarding an issuer for which the Member acted as manager or co-manager of

(i) an initial public offering of equity or equity related securities, for 40 calendar days following the date of the offering; or

(ii) a secondary offering of equity or equity related securities, for 10 calendar days following the date of the offering;

but requirement 14(i) and (ii) do not prevent a Member from issuing a research report concerning the effects of significant news about or a significant event affecting the issuer within the applicable 40 or 10 day period.

14.1. Requirement 14 does not apply where the subject securities are exempted from restrictions under provisions relating to market stabilization in securities legislation or in the Universal Market Integrity Rules.

15. When a Member distributes a research report covering six or more issuers, such a report may indicate where the disclosures required under Policy No. 11 may be found.

16. Members must issue notice of their intention to suspend or discontinue coverage of an issuer. However, no issuance is required when the sole reason for the suspension is that an issuer has been placed on a Member's restricted list.

17. Members must obtain an annual certification from the head of the research department and chief executive officer which states that their analysts are familiar with and have complied with the AIMR Code of Ethics and Standards of Professional Conduct whether they are members of AIMR or not.

18. Where a supervisory analyst of a Member serves as an officer or director of an issuer, then the Member must not provide research on the issuer.

19. Members must pre-approve analysts outside business activities.

20. Where Members set price targets as recommended under guideline 4, Members must disclose the valuation methods used.

## Guidelines

In addition to the above requirements, when establishing policies and procedures as referred to under requirement 1 of Policy No. 11, Members must comply with the following best practices, where practicable:

1. Members should distinguish clearly in each research report between information provided by the issuer or obtained elsewhere and the analyst's own assumptions and opinions.

2. Members should disclose in their research reports and recommendations reliance by the analyst upon any report or study by third party experts other than the analyst responsible for the report. Where there is such reliance, the name of the third party experts should be disclosed.

3. Members should adopt standards of research coverage that include, at a minimum, the obligation to maintain and publish current financial estimates and recommendations on securities followed, and to revisit such estimates and recommendations within a reasonable time following the release of material information by an issuer or the occurrence of other relevant events.

4. Members should set price targets for recommended transactions, where practicable, and with the appropriate disclosure.

5. Members should use specific securities terminology in research reports where required to do so by Securities Legislation. Where such terminology is not required, Members should use the specific technical terminology that is required by the relevant industry, professional association or regulatory authority or in the absence of required terminology use technical terminology that is customarily in use. Where necessary, for full understanding, a glossary should be included.

6. A Member should make its research reports widely available through its websites or by other means for all of its clients whom the Member has determined are entitled to receive such research reports at the same time.

7. Where feasible by virtue of the number of analysts, Members should appoint one or more supervisory analyst or head of research to be responsible for reviewing and approving research reports as required under By-law 29.7, who should be a partner, director or officer of the Member and should have the CFA designation or other appropriate qualifications. Members may have more than one supervisory analyst where necessary.

8. Members should require their analyst employees to obtain the Chartered Financial Analyst designation or other appropriate qualifications.

9. Members should require that the head of the research department, or in small firms where there is no head then the analyst or analysts report to a senior officer or partner who is not the head of the investment banking department. However, no policies or procedures will be approved under requirement 1 unless the Association is satisfied that they address the relationship between the investment-banking department and research department.

CHAPTER

# Institutional
# EQUITY SALES

# CHAPTER 3

# Institutional Equity Sales

## Overview

OF ALL THE JOBS IN THE FINANCIAL COMMUNITY, the institutional equity sales role (also known as *research sales*) is probably the most glamorous and the most sought-after. I don't know if it's the collegial, dynamic atmosphere of the sales/trading desk, or the generous compensation for what some perceive to be easy hours, or having a good-sized expense account with which to entertain institutional clients. Regardless of the reason(s), more research people, investment bankers, and buy-siders look to make a switch to institutional sales than into any other role on the Street.

Come to think of it, there are many examples of successful I-bankers and research analysts who have taken temporary pay cuts just to get a spot on a sales desk. It is virtually unheard of, however, to see an institutional salesperson give up his or her coveted chair in order to go into research or I-banking.

Institutional equity sales is a high profile career that is extremely difficult to break into. Most Canadian brokerage firms prefer to hire experienced institutional salespeople with established client relationships or groom younger talent internally for a junior sales role. And while the local offices of the foreign dealers also have this preference, a couple of global firms do recruit MBA's for junior sales positions.

"People who end up in equity sales should appreciate the importance of the "know your client" rule, have an educated opinion, be trustworthy and conscientious. A good salesperson uses their resources well, is not afraid to ask difficult questions, and thrives on the stress of juggling several balls in the air at once."

—*Kelly Gray, CFA, Institutional Equity Sales, RBC Capital Markets*

## Education

For the most part, institutional sales-people in Canada tend to be generalists. They will talk to one client about an auto parts company on one phone call, then discuss the merits of a certain software company with another client on the next call, and then argue the pros and cons of a biotech firm's new drug on the next call. As such, there are really no hard and fast rules about educational requirements when it comes to institutional salespeople. An understanding of finance and economics is definitely an asset, so having either an undergraduate or graduate degree in either of those disciplines is adequate.

## Compensation Range

Institutional salespeople on Bay Street are compensated on a salary-plus-bonus system. Revenues generated by investment banking and agency trading are allocated to different "pools" and individual bonuses are paid from the pools. With a pool system, there is little transparency in terms of *how* one gets paid. According to some of the more practical folks, however, they don't care *how* they get paid as long as their T4 fairly reflects their efforts.

The tier one dealers typically pay rookie salespeople a base salary of $100,000 and a bonus in the first year of approximately $75,000. The tier two firms may pay a lower base salary of approximately $75,000 and a first year bonus of $25,000–$50,000.

Don't worry too much about the money at the beginning. If you're any good, the money will come.

---

In the old days, institutional salespeople employed at independent investment dealers were paid commissions based on direct drive (eat-what-you-kill) formulas. For example, an institutional boutique's formula would look something like this:

- 16% payout for agency business (trading commissions) from Canadian accounts

- 20% payout for agency business from U.S. accounts

- 10% payout on new issue business if the firm was the lead banker on a deal

- 6% payout on new issue business if the firm was not lead banker on a deal

With a direct drive formula in place, salespeople had transparency in terms of knowing why they were being paid what they were. They simply added up all their commissions and applied the appropriate percentage to calculate their bonuses. The other attractive feature was there was usually no cap on a big producer's earnings—if one brought in the business, one got paid. Today, none of the tier one firms use the direct drive compensation model.

---

## Industry Certification

In order to be a registered representative (an individual licensed to sell securities) in Canada, an individual must pass both the Canadian Securities Course (CSC) and the Conduct and Practices Handbook Course (CPH). The Canadian Securities Course is a straightforward introductory level course that provides a good overview on capital markets and investment products. The Conduct and Practices Handbook Course, on the other hand, is more like reading a rulebook— the rules and regulations of the securities industry, standards of conduct, etc.

To be a registered representative in the U.S. requires state registration. This involves passing two exams as part of state licensing requirements: the Series 63 is the state law test (a test of knowledge about the Uniform Securities Act) for broker-dealer representatives, and the Series 7 Examination is the qualification examination for General Securities Registered Representatives.

As well, having the CFA designation is highly recommended. The CFA designation has become the standard in the investment/finance industry. The program may or may not make you a better salesperson but successful completion of the program has become a rite of passage into the institutional equity community. When one looks around the community, most professionals have the designation, so having it doesn't set you apart—but not having it will.

## The Job

The institutional salesperson's "office" is the fast-paced I-desk (institutional equity sales and trading desk) and is arguably the most dynamic place to be within the firm. However, as the relationship manager between their firm and the institutional investors (the money management firms), salespeople are often out of the office marketing the firm's analysts, taking corporate management teams to see clients, taking clients on site/company visits, or out entertaining clients.

The institutional sales role is that of a relationship manager in that the salesperson serves as a conduit between the firm's products (research and investment banking) and the money managers. To perform the role effectively, a salesperson needs to:

1. **Build and maintain strong relationships with institutional investors (mutual funds, hedge funds, pension funds, insurance companies, etc.).**

   Most good relationships are built on mutual trust and respect and this one is no different. Salespeople that adopt the securities industry's "know your client rule," provide excellent customer service, and take the high road when it comes to professional conduct will gain the trust and respect of clients.

2. **Work at a firm where there is good research and investment banking product.**

   Institutional salespeople need good research and investment banking product to sell to their clients. Good research product means having a number of well-regarded and well-ranked analysts on the research team that the institutional investors consider as "go-to" analysts in their particular industry sector. Good investment banking product means having a constant flow (equity markets permitting) of quality new issues to sell.

   In an ideal world, rookie salespeople should start at a firm with a larger research department. When one is starting out on the I-desk, having more research ideas from more analysts gives you more reasons to talk to your clients and actively build the relationships. Furthermore, having more industry sectors covered by the research team allows one to develop a broader knowledge base. Having said that, most of the larger firms hire their rookie salespeople from within, so another option is to get your start on the desk of a small or mid-sized dealer. The key is to get on a desk and prove yourself.

### 3. Develop deep product knowledge about the firm's products.

Most institutional salespeople must develop an understanding of companies/businesses across a wide range of industry sectors. (There are, however, several Calgary-based energy boutiques whose research coverage is focused on oil and gas companies, oil service companies, pipelines and utilities, and energy trusts. The salespeople at these firms tend to be specialists.) Just as important, if not more so, is understanding the drivers of a company's stock price.

Salespeople that endear themselves to their clients are value-added in that they consistently generate good moneymaking ideas.

"Respect your clients—remember that the (institutional) clients are over-brokered and their time is at a premium...be brief, be concise, be articulate, and be prepared...and remember that contrary opinions are often of highest value."
—*Steve Mantel, CFA, Institutional Equity Sales,*
*National Bank Financial*

Once a new recruit starts on the desk, the first step is to get licensed to sell securities, which involves passing the CSC and CPH to cover Canadian accounts and the Series 7 and 63 to cover U.S. clients. During this licensing period, the new salesperson gets acquainted with the firm's research product by reading the reports on the most topical industries/companies and meeting the firm's research analysts. Once the new recruit is licensed to sell, he or she is assigned a handful of accounts. The firm usually gives the new hire "C" accounts (small accounts that currently don't do a lot of business with the firm) to start with. If the new salesperson does well with those accounts, and as the firm gains confidence in the new recruit's abilities, he or she gets assigned better (more important, higher-volume) accounts as time goes on.

When assigning accounts, firms usually hand out account lists in one of three ways:

1. **By geography**. A salesperson is usually allocated accounts in a given geography. Naturally, the national firms have satellite/branch offices in Montreal, Vancouver, New York, and Boston, and will have one or two salespeople working out of those offices to service institutional investors in those locales. However, some of the smaller independent firms that have their whole desk based in Toronto (or the energy boutiques that have their whole desk based out of Calgary) allocate account coverage by geography to make it logistically simpler when marketing analysts or when taking company managements to see clients.

2. **By account type**. There are two main types of accounts: fundamental and hedge/arbitrage accounts. The two types of accounts have different ways of investing/doing business and therefore it makes sense to have them separated for account coverage purposes. Fundamental accounts are the traditional long-only money managers (being "long" a stock simply means owning the stock). In order to earn commissions from these accounts, a salesperson has to get his firm's resources (analysts, traders, and themselves) voted onto the client's commission list as well as generate money-making investment ideas. On the other hand,

hedge funds tend to be trading accounts and therefore react quickly to, and pay for, good moneymaking investment ideas.

3. **By relationships.** First and foremost, the securities business is a relationship business. Some investment dealers take that to heart in allocating accounts so whichever salesperson has the best relationship with the portfolio managers and analysts at a particular account will cover the account.

At first glance, the institutional sales job seems straightforward enough—to sell the firm's products (research and investment banking) to institutional investors. However, like anything else, there are a number of options in terms of style and approach. On the one end of the spectrum are the generalist salespeople, while on the other end are salespeople who are virtually portfolio managers. And there's any combination of the two in between.

The good generalist salesperson tends to be an extremely effective conduit in managing the flow of information/products to his or her clients—the firm's analysts are effectively marketed to the clients, the firm's research ideas are highlighted to the accounts that would be interested in the companies/industry sectors, meetings with company management teams are consistently arranged, etc.

The virtual portfolio manager-type salespeople are usually former buy-side or sell-side analysts that may know one, or a number of, industries extremely well by virtue of having covered the industry. They tend to spend more of their time "drilling down" into individual stories with their accounts. The trend over the last cycle has clearly been towards recruiting more of this type of salesperson onto the sales desks.

## Getting Started

Institutional equity sales is a high-profile career that is extremely difficult to break into. Most Canadian brokerage firms prefer to hire experienced institutional salespeople with established client relationships or to groom younger talent internally for a junior sales role. And while the local offices of the foreign dealers also have this preference, a couple of global firms do recruit MBAs for junior sales positions.

It is the exception, rather than the rule, to see a young sales candidate recruited straight from MBA school. The most common sources of institutional sales recruits are (listed in order of frequency):

1. **The research associate ranks.** When a spot opens up on the sales desk at one of the larger dealers, it is not uncommon for the head of the desk to look to the research team's pool of associates and give one a shot on the desk. The lucky one will likely be one who has put in their time (minimum of two years as an associate), has worked hard at making their analyst look good, has excellent client interaction skills, is presentable, and has the "gift of the gab."

   There are two reasons why the head of sales would go this route. First, the head of sales gets a "known commodity." He has seen the associate in action, presenting information in the morning meetings in the absence of his or her senior analyst, interacting with peers and senior staffers, exhibiting a sense of urgency in communicating information in his or her industry to the sales/trading desk, etc. Second, it's the firm's way of keeping the associates hungry and staying loyal to the company. By dangling the carrot of future opportunities within the firm for those who excel, management keeps the younger staff motivated and (hopefully) loyal. On the other hand, if the firm were to hire an associate from a competitor for such a coveted spot, the firm runs the risk of shaking the morale and commitment of the firm's own associates who had their sights set on the job.

2. **The research analyst ranks.** Hiring an established research analyst into a sales role has its advantages. First, it is a cost effective way for dealers to hire professionals with account relationships onto their sales desk. All things being equal, the head of sales would rather hire a salesperson with established account relationships, but to successfully poach even an intermediate one (in terms of seniority) or a B-team one (in terms of quality) from a competitor would probably involve paying a minimum guaranteed comp package of a half-million dollars for the first year. Not all I-desks can afford to do that. (It's one thing to pay someone a generous bonus if the markets co-operate and the individual earns it; it's another to guarantee it up front.) Hiring an established analyst, on the other hand, theoretically gives the desk access to that analyst's account relationships with the understanding that the former analyst simply gets a base salary and a cut of the bonus pool, like everybody else on the desk. It is more cost effective. Second, it raises the bar in terms of product knowledge on the desk. While most generalist, non-former analyst salespeople are "a mile wide, an inch deep" when it comes to the knowledge of the various industry sectors, a salesperson with an analyst background will be very fluent in one or two industries. Furthermore, their analytical and research skills will also allow them to drill deeper into stories that are not in their own field of expertise. These attributes give the former analyst an advantage

in talking to money managers in that they can "talk the talk." The desk benefits with the addition of a savvy team member with which they can exchange ideas.

3. **The investment banking teams.** Former I-bankers, with their well-developed financial skills, can bring a different perspective to a sales desk. Furthermore, senior I-bankers will have client management experience (albeit corporate clients rather than institutional clients).

4. **The buy-side.** A few buy-side analysts and portfolio managers have made the switch to institutional sales successfully. Buy-siders, in theory, should be able to make the transition with little difficulty given that they know the companies and the drivers of the stock prices, but the buy-side is not where one learns strong customer service skills (which are absolutely essential on the sell-side and especially in the institutional sales role).

5. **The retail broker ranks.** Several retail brokers have successfully made the move to the institutional desk, since the retail sales experience can be a good training ground for the I-desk. Retail salespeople have acquired the product knowledge and selling skills necessary for the job, but most importantly, they have learned to handle rejection.

6. **The fixed-income sales desk.** A few former institutional bond salesmen have also made the successful transition to equity sales. Their macroeconomic perspective brings a different view to clients. As well, they've had a chance to hone their sales skills in selling a different financial product to a sophisticated audience.

"Spending time in equity research provides an excellent foundation for the institutional sales role. The short term sacrifice provides a long term reward. The clients value experience and perspective and are therefore more receptive to salespeople that have a deeper view than just their firms' written research."

*—Vice president, Institutional Equity Sales*

## A Day in the Life of a Top Institutional Salesperson

**Kelly Gray**, CFA, is an institutional salesperson at RBC Capital Markets. Ms. Gray has been covering institutional accounts for 20 years.

Bachelor of Arts (economics) from University of Western Ontario, 1983

After completing my undergraduate degree in math and economics, I took a summer job as a retail sales assistant at Dominion Securities in a branch office. My learning curve was steep and exciting since I had an unsatiable appetite for more knowledge on how the stock market worked. During my first few months, most of my spare time was spent studying to pass the Canadian Securities course, the options course, and the futures course. I quickly realized, however, that my formal education and the prerequisite securities courses were just a start to having any credibility as a full-fledged stockbroker. It's the skills that one doesn't learn from books that sets you apart in this business: good organizational skills, strong interpersonal skills, patience/perseverance, and a genuine appreciation of the "know your client" rule. Understanding that each client has a different level of knowledge/sophistication with respect to the stock market, and learning to deal with their varied wants and needs, was a great learning experience and gave me some insight into one aspect of being an equity salesperson. Whether in retail or institutional sales, actively applying the "know your client" rule is one of the keys to success.

My next career move took me to South Africa during one of the greatest gold bull markets ever. The gold price ran from US$170/oz in early 1985 to over US$500/oz in 1988. I was fortunate to get a "sink or swim" institutional equity sales job with a small independent broker, Frankel Kruger Inc., at a time when their markets were coming alive. On the floor of the Johannesburg Stock Exchange, I learned how to trade equities and truly began to understand what moved markets, again realizing that the most important information could not be learned from textbooks.

Through networking in South Africa, I met my future employer (Burns Fry) and I moved back to Canada to sell Canadian equities to U.S. institutional money managers. This was a phenomenal learning experience in terms of learning how to make an effective sales call. Prospecting became a fine art and perfecting a sales call was a necessity. Catching the interest of the portfolio manager/analyst was not an easy task. Selling into the domestic market is similar, but easier in that your audience is focused on Canadian stocks. The challenge in selling to "experts" in the Canadian market was finding the incremental or red flag information that helped them to make an investment decision, versus the U.S. money managers who wanted to know the five key reasons to look at the company and how it compared to their global competitors.

I find that every day is different and exciting on the institutional equity sales desk. The opportunities are endless, your knowledge base grows daily. You feel like you have your finger on the pulse of whatever is happening not only in the stock market, but also in the world of politics and economics, different industry developments, technology, natural disasters, and even events in your own community. There is very little that cannot be tied to stock markets. You are a generalist with access to specialists and experts in their fields, you're exposed to a broad group of personality types, and you can entertain clients at sporting events, the opera, musicals, charity events, and the newest restaurants. I would say my attraction to this job today is still the same or greater than it was when I took the summer job as a retail assistant so long ago. The difference is that today, I have a much better appreciation for what the job is all about!

My typical day as an institutional salesperson might look like this:

**6:00 a.m.**   My day begins with reading the business newspapers at home, checking my RIM pager, and listening to "CNN News" for any new events unfolding.

**6:45 a.m.**   Once at the office, I go through and respond to my e-mails, read the Canadian morning research notes, scan the U.S. morning research notes, and prepare for the Institutional Equity Sales/Trading and Research morning meeting.

**7:30 a.m.**   My participation in the morning meetings includes questioning the traders about the market flows and the analysts about any developments in their industry sectors that may affect their research recommendations. In the sales portion of the meeting, the sales group is updated on the current status of corporate finance deals and highlights/ feedback from recent company visits or new issue meetings.

**8:15 a.m.**   Head back to my desk to make my morning calls to my clients. Before I pick up the phone, I e-mail out our morning trading comments, our Canadian morning meeting summary comments, and our U.S. morning meeting summary comments. I try to recap the most important information from our morning meetings in a succinct call. All portfolio managers and buy-side analysts are inundated with calls in the morning so you want your call to have the most value-added content that pertains to their investment style and portfolios.

**8:30 a.m.**  Call portfolio manager X with an overview of stocks covered this morning and to follow up on the consumer products company/stock she has been doing work on. I get her voicemail, so I leave a message.

**8:40 a.m.**  Call another one of my Toronto-based accounts to give him some feedback from yesterday afternoon's management visit with auto parts company A that he couldn't attend, and tie in our current recommendation on company A and our view on the sector. I mention we are a seller of company A stock on the trading desk.

**9:05 a.m.**  Call portfolio manager Y with comments from our top-ranked healthcare analyst regarding his interpretations of the recent clinical trial results. The fund manager wants to dig deeper, so I conference the analyst in.

**9:30 a.m.**  Call the senior resource analyst at my pension fund client to discuss the NAV estimate revisions that our top-ranked oil analyst made this morning. Although the revisions were on the morning meeting summary comments that I e-mailed out, I want to highlight the companies they own and how they are impacted, or companies they don't own that look interesting.

**9:50 a.m.**  One of my sales colleagues is waiting for me in the lobby of his client's building with the management team of the technology company whose IPO we're leading. After brief introductions, the other salesperson heads back to the office while I take the management team to see one of my clients. (It's important for the sales group to work together and to be considerate of everyone's time. These marketing schedules are very tight and it is imperative that the meetings start and finish on time.)

**11:15 a.m.**   Head over to another dealer's office for a dry run of an income trust IPO they are leading.

**11:25 a.m.**   Finish off morning calls and answer e-mails.

**12:00 p.m.**   Today we're hosting a client luncheon with management from a senior gold company so I go over to the boardroom and chat with my clients that are attending. Once the meeting gets underway, I go back to the desk for a sandwich; the lunchtime gives me an opportunity to speak to analysts, deal with administrative tasks, and get caught up with the traders that are working on some of my clients' orders.

**2:15 p.m.**   Sales/trading/research conference call to review activity flows in the market, updates on company news from the morning, and stocks to focus on for the afternoon.

**2:30 p.m.**   Take our income trust analyst across the street to see portfolio manager Z.

**3:30 p.m.**   I use this time to book company and analyst meetings and to confirm my meetings for the next day. I check my e-mail inbox, return phone calls, and sort through the day's research.

**4:00 p.m.**   Market closes.

**4:15 p.m.**   I (along with the rest of the sales desk) attend another "teach in" where analysts focus on a specific investment idea, a new research report, a new technology, or revisit an old recommendation, or we do a dry run with our analyst for an upcoming new issue.

**5:15 p.m.** Put aside a research report just published by our real estate analyst and a newsletter, both to be read later tonight. Return a couple more phone calls and check my schedule, one last time, for the next day.

**5:45 p.m.** Head home to be with my family (but also regularly go out to the newest hot restaurants with clients and colleagues).

## HOW INSTITUTIONAL SALESPEOPLE SPEND THEIR TIME

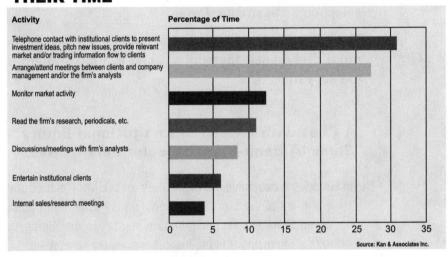

The above percentages tend to change depending on:

- **A salesperson's location relative to his or her clients.** The location of a salesperson relative to his or her clients will affect the amount of time spent on client entertainment. For example, salespeople located in Canadian offices with account coverage responsibilities in the U.S. allocate less of their time to client entertainment than salespeople located where their clients are.

- **The type/size of firm the salesperson works for**. The larger the firm, the bigger the research department. The domestic bank-owned investment dealers have between 20 and 30 industry analysts in their research department, while the mid-sized independent firms have approximately 15 analysts, and the small independent firms have less than 10 analysts. Therefore, salespeople that work for the larger bank-owned dealers tend to spend more of their time marketing analysts (and company management teams) than do salespeople at smaller firms.

- **The quality of the analysts**. The better the analysts, the more likely a salesperson is going to market them to the accounts.

## A Chat with a Head of Institutional Equity Sales (A Bank-Owned Dealer Perspective)

**David Fleck** is an executive managing director at BMO NesbittBurns and head of the firm's institutional equity sales and trading group. Prior to assuming management responsibilities, he was a key member of the institutional equity sales team.

Q. **BMO Nesbitt Burns is recognized as having one of the strongest sales/trading desks on the street. What do you attribute that to?**

A. It's a combination of two factors:

1. The right client interface. We try as best as we can to have the right fit (between the salesperson and the institutional client) in assigning accounts to our salespeople and we're sensitive to making any required changes quickly. This requires frequent contact and feedback from our institutional clients, so I make a point of doing

account reviews with a cross-section of our top 25 to 30 accounts in North America on an annual basis.

2. The right mix of salespeople and traders. If you look across our sales/trading team, you'll see a good mix and balance of experience levels, gender, age, and account relationships. Our clients are diverse so our team should be set up to reflect that diversity.

**Q. What is your philosophy behind account coverage?**

A. Our top 10 accounts in Canada all have been assigned multiple sales coverage. In other words, there are two, and in some cases three, salespeople covering our highest commission-paying clients. The fit between the salesperson and the portfolio managers/analysts is also key.

**Q. As head of sales, what attributes do you look for when hiring a salesperson?**

A. When I'm hiring an inexperienced equity salesperson, I usually look at the internal candidates (from research or investment banking) with the best interpersonal skills and the best cultural fit with the other members of our sales team. I tend to take the technical skills for granted because they wouldn't be with us (NesbittBurns) otherwise. So I focus on the interpersonal skills because this is a people business and unless people want to talk to you, it really doesn't matter how smart you are.

**Q. What distinguishes a successful salesperson from others that are less so?**

A. The successful salespeople have the ability to connect well with clients. Also, the ability to combine good analytical skills with strong interpersonal skills is very important. There are many salespeople with good interpersonal skills but average analytical skills and sometimes vice versa.

That's why there are lots of good salespeople but very few great salespeople.

**Q. Was there any experience that helped shape your sales career?**

A. I would say that my varied experiences (academic, work, and life experiences) have helped to differentiate me.

**Q. What is the biggest misconception of the institutional sales job?**

A. Most people don't appreciate how hard it is to get someone (e.g., an overbrokered portfolio manager) to take or return your phone call. But you have to find a way, an angle, and that's where the psychology of selling comes into play. Effective sales in our business of selling intangibles is probably only about 50% content; the other 50% is understanding client preferences.

**Q. When making a new hire for the desk after a salesperson has left, how important is the account fit?**

A. Account fit is just one of the factors we would take into consideration. From the perspective of a bank-owned dealer/platform, we are not simply trying to maximize our commission revenues this quarter or the next. We are trying to build a franchise (for the next 10 to 15 years) that will dominate the industry across a number of measures. So again, we look at the cultural fit. And I don't mean simply how well the potential candidates get along with our existing team. We want to make sure the team is balanced in terms of the age dynamic, the gender dynamic, and that we've got an optimum mix of experienced versus less experienced salespeople.

**Q.  What advice would you give to a rookie institutional sales-person?**

A.  New junior hires on a sales desk are often pressured to do a trade. I tell my new recruits not to even talk about doing a trade with a client while the relationship is still being established. You have to build the trust first, establish a bond. Let the trader talk to the client's trader about doing trades. Clients often believe that salespeople are looking to do a trade so it's your job to convince them that you're not, that you're there to provide service and information flow and access to your firm's resources.

### Profile of the Ideal Institutional Equity Sales Candidate

The ideal institutional sales candidate should have the following attributes:

- proven selling skills
- strong interpersonal skills
- be a good listener
- personality—the ability to build and maintain strong client relationships
- an excellent customer service ethic
- good product knowledge
- good market sense
- strong sense of urgency
- tenacity
- an interest and understanding of financial markets

"If you want to be a good salesperson, you have to first learn to be a good listener."

—*Tim Brown, CFA, Institutional Equity Sales,*
*RBC Capital Markets*

## The 10 Largest Institutional Equity Sales Teams in Canada*

| Company | Number of Team Members |
|---|---|
| 1. CIBC World Markets | 24 |
| 2. RBC Capital Markets | 21 |
| 3. UBS Securities | 21 |
| 4. BMO Nesbitt Burns | 18 |
| 5. National Bank Financial | 17 |
| 6. TD Newcrest | 15 |
| 7. Scotia Capital | 15 |
| 8. GMP Securities | 14 |
| 9. Raymond James Canada | 13 |
| 10. Desjardins Securities | 11 |

*Measured by number of salespeople based in North America selling Canadian and/or U.S. research product.

## Suggested Reading

1. *Art of Selling Intangibles* (by LeRoy Gross, published by Prentice Hall Press)

   Written by LeRoy Gross, a former top retail sales producer who later managed the sales development and training programs for a Wall Street brokerage firm, this book packages his many practical sales strategies and techniques.

2. *The Excellent Investment Advisor* (by Nick Murray, published by The Nick Murray Company)

   This book is considered a "must read" by many financial advisors.

3. *Handbook of Canadian Security Analysis, Volumes I & II* (edited by Joe Kan, published by John Wiley & Sons)

   This valuable reference is a guide to evaluating the industry sectors of the market. Some 28 of Canada's top-ranked sell-side analysts were hand-picked to share their expertise and experience in understanding and analyzing the fundamental forces that drive stock performance in each industry group.

4. *How to Make Hot Cold Calls: Your Calling Card to Personal Success* (by Steven J. Schwartz, published by Stoddart)

   The author offers practical insights to those looking for guidance on how to market over the phone and effectively communicate the value of a good or service to prospects and clients.

5. *How to Win Friends and Influence People* (by Dale Carnegie, published by Simon and Schuster)

   One of the best-selling books of all-time, this book addresses a universal challenge: Getting along with and influencing people in both a social and business context. This is the primary text used in the Dale Carnegie Courses in Effective Speaking and Human Relations.

6. *Manias, Panics and Crashes: A History of Financial Crises* (by Charles P. Kindleberger, published by John Wiley & Sons)

   This is the most popular of 30 books published by Charles Kindleberger, financial historian and former Ford Professor of Economics at MIT. This is a classic on the theme of irrational behaviour and speculation in the financial markets.

7. *Markets, Mobs and Mayhem: A Cultural History of the Madness of Crowds* (by Robert Menschel, published by John Wiley & Sons)

   The author, a senior director of the Goldman Sachs Group, provides witty accounts and insights into crowd behaviour and financial speculation.

8. *The Power of Focus: How to Hit Your Business, Personal and Financial Targets with Absolute Certainty* (by Jack Canfield, et al., published by Health Communications)

   The authors of the *Chicken Soup for the Soul* series outline 10 "focusing strategies" that they used to build their business.

9. *SPIN Selling* (by Neil Rackham, published by McGraw-Hill)

   This book is targeted at salespeople that sell high-value goods or services to sophisticated buyers. The author draws interesting real-world examples and cases from over a decade of research into the sales process.

10. *The Tao of Sales: The Easy Way to Sell in Tough Times* (by E. Thomas Behr, et al., published by Harper Collins UK)

    Taoist principles applied to the sales process and client relationship management.

11. *True Professionalism: The Courage to Care About Your People, Your Clients, and Your Career* (by David H. Maister, published by Free Press)

    The author, a consultant to professional service firms, addresses the concept of professionalism at both the individual and company level. He offers practical advice on continual professional self-improvement and being client-focused.

12. *Wine Spectator's Essentials of Wine: A Guide to the Basics* (by Harvey Steiman, published by Running Press)

    A "must read" for any institutional salesperson.

CHAPTER 4

# Institutional
# EQUITY TRADER

CHAPTER 4

# Institutional
# Equity Trader

## Overview

THE INSTITUTIONAL EQUITY TRADING DESK is typically staffed
with two types of traders: agency traders (also known as *coverage traders* or *sales traders*) and liability traders (also known
as *capital traders* or *facilitation traders*). Agency traders execute
block trades for institutional clients, while liability traders
assist in facilitating client trades by committing and managing the firm's trading capital.

For either role, having street smarts and the ability to
think on one's feet, and being able to work under pressure,
are much more valued attributes than in most of the other
jobs profiled in this book. Furthermore, having a passion for
the financial markets is crucial—you will live, eat, and
breathe stocks well before the markets open and long after
they close. Once you're in the business, the majority of your
social circle will be other Bay Streeters and just about every
conversation will be dominated by "shop talk."

Institutional equity trading is a high-pressure career that is
extremely difficult to break into. Most Canadian brokerage
firms prefer to hire experienced institutional traders with
established client relationships, or groom younger talent
internally for a junior trading role. And while the local offices

**EDUCATION**
Undergraduate and/or graduate degree in finance/economics

**COMPENSATION RANGE**
$100,000 – $1 million plus

**INDUSTRY CERTIFICATION**
CFA designation recommended

Canadian Securities Course required

Conduct and Practices Handbook Course required

Uniform Securities Agent State Law Examination (Series 63) required for U.S. client coverage

General Securities Registered Representative Examination (NASD Series 7) required for U.S. client coverage

TSX Trader's Training Course

of foreign dealers also have this preference, a couple of global firms do recruit MBAs for junior trading positions.

## Education

For the most part, institutional equity traders in Canada are similar to salespeople in that they tend to be generalists. They will talk to one client (typically a buy-side trader but sometimes the portfolio manager) about an oil company's stock on one phone call, then discuss the market action of a certain telecom stock with another client on the next call, and move on to discuss a mining company's stock on the following call. As such, there are really no hard and fast rules about educational requirements when it comes to institutional equity traders. An understanding of finance and economics is definitely an asset, so having an undergraduate or graduate degree in either of those disciplines is adequate.

## Compensation Range

Institutional equity traders on Bay Street are compensated on a salary-plus-bonus system. Revenues generated by investment banking and agency trading are allocated to different "pools," from which individual bonuses are paid.

The tier one dealers typically pay rookie traders a base salary of $100,000 and a bonus in the first year of approximately $75,000. The tier two firms may pay a lower base salary of approximately $75,000 and a first-year bonus of $25,000 to $50,000.

Don't worry too much about the money at the beginning—just get your foot in the door. If you're any good, the money will come.

## Industry Certification

In order to cover institutional accounts in Canada on a trading basis, an individual must pass both the Canadian Securities Course (CSC) and the Conduct and Practices Handbook Course (CPH). The Canadian Securities Course is a straightforward introductory-level course that provides a good overview on capital markets and investment products. The Conduct and Practices Handbook Course, on the other hand, is more like reading a rulebook—the rules and regulations of the securities industry, standards of conduct, etc.

Covering accounts in the U.S. requires state registration. This involves passing two exams as part of state licensing requirements: the Series 63 Exam is the state law test (a test of knowledge about the Uniform Securities Act) for broker-dealer representatives, and the Series 7 Examination is the qualification examination for General Securities Registered Representatives.

As well, having the CFA designation is highly recommended. The CFA designation has become the standard in the investment/finance industry. The program may or may not make you a better trader but successful completion of the program has become a rite of passage into the institutional equity community.

## Relevant Trading Terminology

Bid: the price that a buyer is willing to pay. In the context of a quote on a stock (i.e., the bid and the ask), the bid is the highest price that any buyer is willing to pay at that particular moment.

The book: the trading capital employed by a firm for liability/ facilitation purposes.

Good fill: a well-executed order; getting the client the best price.

Hit the bid: sell stock at the bid price.

Indication: a potential order. For example, a trader may be playing golf with a client (the portfolio manager and the buy-side trader). During the course of the game, the portfolio manager reveals that he's overweight the oil & gas sector and double overweight exploration & production (E&P) company ABC, but is getting very nervous about the sustainability of oil prices. The trader now has an *indication* that the client could be a potential seller of E&P company ABC's stock.

Liquidity: the ease with which one can trade in and out of a stock without impacting the market or losing money because of a wide spread between the bid and ask prices. Liquidity is a function of the average daily trading volume on a stock— the higher the volume, the more liquid the stock. One indicator of the liquidity of a stock is simply the spread between the bid and ask prices of that stock—the wider the spread, the less liquid the stock.

Loss ratio: the ratio of a firm's liability capital losses relative to the agency commissions generated. On Bay Street, targeted loss ratios hover around 15%, whereas the targeted loss ratios on Wall Street tend to be higher. Loss ratios are calculated on the firm's overall trading capital, or can be broken down by specific stocks or individual accounts.

Natural buyer/seller: a client order as opposed to employing the firm's trading capital.

Nickel business: the business of buying and selling stocks for institutional clients at two, three, four, or five cents a share in commission.

Offering: the price a seller is willing to sell at. The offering is simply the "ask" side of the stock quote and is the lowest price where any seller is willing to sell at that particular moment.

Overhang: a big block of stock that the market knows is for sale. The price of a stock tends to stagnate if there is over-hang since market participants perceive it to be excess supply.

Penalty box: when an institutional client stops doing business/trade with an investment dealer. This can be temporary or permanent. In the business, it's referred to as being "cut off."

Print: a (block) trade that is successfully executed and has hit the tickertape.

Protection: a courtesy call that a trader owes his or her client if that client has given the trader an indication to buy or sell a certain stock. For example, if a client tells a trader "I'd be a buyer of stock CDE further down, keep me up," and the trader's desk finds a seller, and then another buyer emerges, the trader owes the original potential buyer a call before doing the trade.

Resistance: the level of a stock's price where there are lots of sellers.

Subject order: a "soft" order or an order with a condition. For example, there may be a large block of stock XYZ for sale. A client may want to be long the stock but does not want to buy, knowing there is a size seller in the marketplace. The client may tell the trader who is putting a block together, "I'd be a buyer of 100,000 if a print goes up." Therefore, the client's buy order is subject to the trader finding enough other buyers to collectively buy the seller's large block.

Support: the level of a stock's price where there are lots of buyers.

Take out the offering: buy stock at the offering/ask price.

VWAP (value weighted average price): a benchmark used by buy-side traders to quantify execution costs. Clients may give a broker an order but ask that the broker guarantee that the order is filled at the VWAP. The client then ensures that he or she is buying stock at the day's average price.

## The Job of an Agency Trader

Simply put, the role of an agency trader is to manage and execute the order flow from institutions with minimal market impact, disseminate market intelligence (and any other relevant information) to clients, and manage the trading relationship with their accounts. But the job is harder than it looks—much harder. Just doing the job at a minimal acceptable level means paying attention to a myriad of information sources, being aware of client intentions, watching for and disseminating news that may affect the stocks that clients are trading, giving clients "good fills" on their orders, etc. There are very many moving parts, so the potential to err is enormous. To be a good trader, one must also be able to add value to the client, develop and maintain strong client relationships, and create trading ideas to generate commissions for the firm.

"One of our jobs is to supply good market intelligence (both on the general market as well as on specific stocks) to your buy-side counterparts to make them look good to the portfolio managers."

—*Seasoned Agency Trader*

A good agency trader must:

1. **Pay attention to the various information sources.**

   Most traders will read (or at least grab the headlines from) both of the Canadian business newspapers as well as *The Wall Street Journal* and possibly *The New York Times* as part of their morning routine. Furthermore, on every trader's desk sits a number of terminals or screens that display market and specific stock information: CNBC, the real-time news services (Bloomberg, Reuters, Dow Jones News Service), the major and sub-indices, commodity prices, the ticker tape, the day's top stories, the day's most active stocks, etc. A number of traders also have favourite websites (TheStreet.com, Briefing.com, StockCharts.com, TheGartmanLetter.com, TurtleTrader.com, etc.) that give further colour on market events. Most traders also have their own network of contacts around the Street with which they share information. Paying attention to, and digesting, all the available information serves two purposes:

   • Having a good market sense means having the whole picture, and to get the whole picture one needs to be tuned into every available piece of potentially material information.

   • With the trading function as event-driven as it is, a news item on a given industry or stock that could trigger a trade idea could come across the screen at any moment.

## 2. Be aware of client intentions.

The cardinal rule for every professional on the sell side is the "know-your-client" rule, and this certainly applies to traders as well.

## 3. Watch for, and disseminate, news that may affect the stocks that clients are trading.

For example, if an industry bellwether company (let's say Lucent) were to issue a news release warning of an earnings shortfall in the upcoming quarter, a trader sitting on a client order to buy a block of Nortel should call his or her client and inform them of the Lucent news and its potentially negative impact on the price of Nortel. The trader and the client could then discuss alternative strategies for buying the Nortel position.

## 4. Give clients "good fills" on their orders.

The larger institutions and/or the more active trading accounts may have a large number of big orders on any given trading day. It would not be possible for the in-house trader to single-handedly monitor and execute all the positions with optimum results, so institutions farm out the orders to the brokers they think will do the best job of trading specific stocks and getting the client the best price.

The opposite of giving a client a good fill would be to "fill and bill." For example, a trader gets an order to buy half a million stock STU. She gets a seller of 200,000 and puts up the trade. Once the trade hits the tape, a number of other sellers emerge such that there is more stock for sale than the 300,000 balance of the original buy order. The trader could "fill and bill" by crossing 300,000 right away. Or she could call the buyer back, tell them that there are now several (possibly big) sellers and that they should sit back and nibble away as the stock comes to them and therefore possibly fill the balance of the order at lower prices.

Another example of not getting a client a good fill is when a trader poorly handles a trade. For example, a trader gets an order from a client to buy one million shares of BCD (assume that BCD trades between one and two million shares a day). He announces the order to the rest of the trading desk and every agency trader starts picking up the phone and telling their clients "I'm a buyer of a million BCD." With that kind of demand in the market, sellers on the board would cancel their offerings and the stock would run away. Other buyers may even show up. The client would not likely get a good fill in this situation.

## 5. Be able to add value to the client.

Every good trader is a student of the market. They have taken the time and made the effort to try and understand the dynamics of the market: the psychology, momentum, and sentiment of both individual stocks and the market as a whole. During each trading session, they are able to encapsulate their observations of macroeconomic events and how these events could impact market action, and along with highlights of their firm's research and relevant gossip/scuttlebutt, package and present it in a timely and usable sound bite to their clients.

While traders can be further value-added to their clients by making them money (generating at least a few good money-making ideas each quarter), they can also add value by getting clients out of names/stocks they shouldn't be in.

Here's an example of a good money-making idea: Leading up to an FOMC meeting, the market was expecting the Fed to raise interest rates by a quarter of a point. The same day as the FOMC meeting, Cisco was to report their quarterly results after the close. Trader A had noted that the CEO tends to be cautious or even bearish when giving forward guidance to the Street on his company's financial performance. (The CEO has tempered guidance for the last several quarters.) The trader also noted that the sentiment of the market was skittish—market participants saw the glass as half empty. The trader called his clients and told them that if the Fed raised rates by a quarter point as the market expected, the market would rally. The trader recommended selling into the rally before the close, since the Cisco earnings release after the close would likely spook the already tenuous market.

"Clients do their own homework on the individual stocks and you have to respect that. Our job as traders is to get the big picture right and share that perspective with the client."

—*Brian Clouse, Institutional Equity Trader,*
*Wellington West Capital Markets*

### 6. Develop and maintain strong client relationships.

The institutional equity business is very much a relationship game. The professionals that succeed most are those who are trustworthy, knowledgeable market participants and have their clients' best interests at heart.

### 7. Create trading ideas to generate commissions for the firm.

This is a two-step process:

1. Create the trading idea.

2. Make the trade happen by talking clients into doing the trade.

There are a number of reasons why an institutional account would trade with a given dealer:

1. to pay the firm for good research ideas

2. to pay the firm its commission allocation as determined by the client's internal voting system

3. some accounts simply go where the flow is (i.e., to whichever firm is trading the stock that day)

4. the portfolio manager and/or buy-side trader has a personal relationship with the trader that covers them. They go to the traders they trust and where they know they'll be taken care of

From a business point of view, one of the challenges of an agency trader is to get more commissions from a client than is allocated to the trader's firm by that client's structured commission allocation formula. Beyond the commissions allocated to each individual dealer, every institutional client has some discretionary commissions to pay out to the Street. It is the trader's job to win this discretionary business.

### Breaking onto the Trading Desk as an Agency Trader

In the old days when trading was done on the floor of the Toronto Stock Exchange, young recruits in the trading world paid their dues by starting out as phone clerks, post clerks, or runners, and worked their way up to a trading position. Today, potential young traders pay their dues by spending a couple of years working as a research associate, on the trading desk as a trading assistant, or in a department like stock lending before getting a shot on the trading desk.

## The Job of a Liability Trader

Whereas the role of an agency trader is to manage and execute the order flow from institutions with minimal market impact, the role of a liability trader is to manage the firm's trading capital in order to facilitate those client orders, while losing as little of the firm's trading capital as possible. Liability traders are typically assigned sectors of the market, so one trader on the liability desk may trade the resource sectors/stocks, while another trades tech and biotech names, and so on. The liability trader also plays quarterback in setting direction for the agency traders.

So where an agency trader spends the bulk of their time talking to their trading counterparts on the buy side, liability traders have lighter or no formal institutional account coverage responsibilities. At the domestic bank-owned dealers and the Canadian offices of large global dealers, liability traders typically have no formal account coverage responsibilities, whereas liability traders at the independent firms tend to cover a handful of accounts (usually not more than five). Liability traders, on the other hand, will more likely have relationships with corporate clients. (At small- and even mid-cap public companies, the bulk of management's own net worth is often tied up in company stock, so market perspective on the company's shares is appreciated.)

One of the bigger challenges for liability traders is to maintain a balance between market share and profitability (while keeping in mind the advertising aspect) when employing their capital. On the one hand, strong market share in a given sector or individual stock helps drive investment banking business in that sector or stock (as explained below), but capturing that market share will likely cost the firm some of its trading capital. The other benefit (the advertising aspect) of being active in trading a particular name/stock is the domino effect of putting up trades. Basically, clients see a broker trading a stock that they are looking to trade and will go to that broker for a market. It's the old adage "business begets business."

A goal of liability traders is to be the "go to" dealer on a number of stocks. To do this, they must have the number one market share in each of those stocks. They need to know their sectors and the stocks in their sectors inside and out. They should know which clients play in their sectors and whether they are over- or underweight. They should have a feel for the sentiment in the sectors so they can anticipate rotation into or out of the sector.

### How a Firm Determines the Amount of Trading Capital to Use on the Desk

1. **Look at the universe of stocks that the firm wants to trade.** This is somewhat dictated by the type/size of the firm. For example, the domestic bank-owned dealers tend to play in the large-cap space, whereas the independents focus on the small- and mid-cap companies. It is also dictated by the firm's platform (or business strategy). For example, there are several independent boutiques in Calgary that focus on energy stocks.

2. **Look at the universe of stocks that the firm wants to dominate.** Look at the companies where the firm believes there's potential for investment-banking business. The "nickel business" is sometimes used as a loss leader in order to get participation in equity underwritings/deals. For example, a brokerage firm will aggressively trade company XYZ's stock with the intention of becoming the number one or

two trader in that name. With that status in hand, the brokerage firm can more effectively pitch to be the lead underwriter for the company's next equity financing. The firm's pitch sounds something like this: "As the top trader for your stock, we have the best information on your stock. We know where all the buyers and sellers are. We know how to price the deal and do the deal better than any of our competitors."

3. **Look at average block sizes and average volumes (of the stocks of the companies with potential investment banking business) required to maintain flow.**

4. **Take into consideration the amount of liability capital that competitor firms are employing on their trading desks.**

5. **Review the profitability of the recent month or current month.** If the liability book has been taking losses, a liability trader may rein in his use of trading capital.

### Employing the Capital

There are two ways for a liability trader to use the firm's capital: reactively or proactively.

#### Example of Using Capital Reactively

1. **To facilitate trade for the firm's top institutional accounts.**

If a good client calls the trading desk looking to sell 300 stock ABC on the offering, then the desk will be long 300 stock ABC. If the market on stock ABC is $3.10 to $3.20, then the liability desk (using the firm's capital) is long 300,000 shares at $3.20. The liability trader then turns around and tries to sell the stock. Assuming the market doesn't move, the trader sells all 300,000 shares at $3.10. The trade just cost the firm $30,000 less any commissions taken in on the trade.

*Examples of Using Capital Proactively*

## 1. To support stock calls/recommendations made by the firm's analysts.

The firm's financial services analyst comes out with a "strong buy" on mutual fund company XYZ's stock. The analyst is pounding the table—the company is showing good inflow numbers, the stock trades at a discount multiple to its peers, and there is potential that the company will be taken out. The stock is illiquid. The firm's liability trader starts buying stock on the offering and continues to take out the offering until he finds resistance. Ideally, at that point, one of the sellers calls the liability trader (or one of the agency traders at the firm) and reveals that he/she has a block of stock to sell.

At the same time, the analyst and the salespeople solicit buy orders for mutual fund company XYZ's stock. The firm now has stock to sell to the client because the liability trader was accumulating stock.

## 2. To get in the traffic of an active stock.

Early in a trading session, gold stock ABC is very active and heavily traded. The liability trader's firm doesn't have a gold analyst and is not in the information flow. The trader, however, still wants to get in the traffic, so he tells his agency traders to "go out as a seller of 200 gold stock ABC on the bid" meaning "tell the accounts that we've got 200,000 gold stock ABC for sale at the bid price."

3. **To create trade in stocks/companies where the firm believes there's potential for corporate finance business.**

   Underwriting equity deals is a high margin business. The agency trading commissions helps a brokerage firm keep the lights on but the real money is in doing the deals. Therefore, investment dealers will use/risk liability capital to dominate the trading in a company's stock in order to get participation in that company's equity underwritings/deals. For example, a brokerage firm will aggressively trade company XYZ's stock with the intention of becoming the top trader in that name. With that status in hand, the brokerage firm can more effectively pitch to be the lead underwriter for the company's next equity financing.

There may also be times when there is a good trading idea but the liability trader chooses not to use capital because the risk of losing money is too high. For example, the firm's utilities analyst has a "buy" recommendation on stock DEF because he or she doesn't believe that interest rates are going up as much as the market thinks. Meanwhile, power prices are increasing, and there's an attractive dividend yield. The liability trader looks at the chart on stock DEF and notes that it is oversold on a technical basis and is therefore due for a bounce. The analyst has managed to pull a buy order, but the liability trader chooses not to short stock to the client because it's not worth losing 50 cents a share (when the stock bounces as anticipated) to make 5 cents a share in commissions. The liability trader reflects his thoughts to the agency traders so they look for a natural seller.

### Breaking onto the Trading Desk as a Liability Trader

At the domestic bank-owned investment dealers and the Canadian offices of the large global dealers, there are typically three to five liability traders on the institutional trading desk. At the independent dealers, there are usually only one or two liability traders. In other words, there may be a total of only 50 liability trading spots in the whole country.

On the rare occasion, a dealer has hired an inexperienced individual straight onto the trading desk as a junior liability trader. Typically, however, getting one of those 50 spots is something an individual works up to. Most liability traders evolved into this role after several years of experience as an agency trader.

## A Chat with a Senior Institutional Equity Trader

**Glen Grossmith** is director of institutional trading and a senior agency trader at UBS Securities Canada. He has been a trader for 25 years and was most recently a trader at National Bank Financial with both liability and account coverage responsibilities.

**Q.** **Were you one of these people with an early fascination with the stock market?**

**A.** Somewhat. I had bought shares in Maple Leaf Gardens and a few junior mining companies over a ten year period. In fact, when I graduated with an undergraduate degree in economics from McMaster, I still wasn't sure what career path to pursue. So I decided to stay in school. My intention was to go to MBA school.

**Q.  So did you go to MBA school?**

A.  No. Fate took over. After graduating from McMaster, I needed to sell some of my stock holdings to pay for my continuing education, so I called my broker at Davidson Partners (which was later taken over by Midland Walwyn, which was then bought by Merrill Lynch). The head of retail sales picked up the phone. He asked me why I wanted to sell my stocks. I told him I needed the money to go to MBA school. His response was "Now what do you want to do that for? Why don't you come down to the office and we'll have a chat."

After meeting with the branch manager, he offered me a job as a retail stockbroker. When I showed up for the retail sales training program, they sent me to work down on the floor of the Toronto Stock Exchange as a phone clerk. After three months, I started writing trade tickets and started liking the job. I was watching some pretty regular guys having fun and making good money. After six months, I started trading orders. After two years, I became what was called a Registered Trader (RT) in those days. After 13 years as an RT on the floor, I moved up to the institutional desk at First Marathon (the predecessor firm to National Bank Financial) as a liability trader.

**Q.  So do you have any regrets about not going to MBA school?**

A.  Maybe during those first couple of months on the floor when I was making an annualized salary of $9,800 (just about all my classmates were making at least double that). Then as I started trading, I found that it was stimulating and fun, and I was getting the same adrenaline rush from trading that I got from playing sports. I didn't think you could get that from the business world.

**Q. You started your institutional trading career trading liability. Do you think that gives you an advantage as an agency trader?**

A. Absolutely. I think trading liability helped me get a better feel for the market. I picked up on what news and economic numbers affect stocks. I learned where the support levels were on certain stocks. These are things that a liability trader learns because he's constantly trading, whereas being an agency trader, you only trade when you get an order. And because most liability traders are assigned certain sectors, you become very knowledgeable about the stocks in your sector(s) over time.

**Q. What characteristics/abilities should a good agency trader have?**

A. First, one should be able to read the market. Second, know your client. Listen to what your client wants. Third, service the client. Take advantage of your firm's resources (research, sales, etc.) to personalize your service according to what the client wants. Some clients want specific information on specific stocks. Then that's what you give them. Other clients only want to be called with good money-making ideas. Then that's what you give *them*. Fourth, like most other relationships, it comes down to trust. Clients prefer to do business with people they trust. Fifth, make your clients (typically the buy-side traders) look good in front of their boss(es) (the portfolio managers). As an example, we had an order on the desk the other day to buy company XYZ. Our analyst told us that the Street's numbers (the range of earnings estimates from our competitors) were too high. Then the company announced that they will delay reporting their quarterly numbers, which is never a good sign. So we told the client not to buy the stock. Shortly afterwards, the company reported their quarter and it turned out that there was accounting fraud. The stock's now down 30%. Our client (the trader) looked pretty good on that one.

**Q.  You've worked at several platforms—an independent dealer, a bank-owned dealer, and now a global dealer. From a trading perspective, do you see an advantage to being at a global dealer?**

A.  Definitely. I think I see much more information and (trade) flow than my competitors at domestic shops. UBS is one of the top traders of Canadian equities in North America. Having access to the firm's global research is a huge bene-fit. Furthermore, our Canadian trading desk is linked to our large U.S. trading desk, so we manage to get a good feel for flow in most North American stocks. One sector that I believe we have a competitive advantage in is mining—all the firm's trading in North American mining names is done on our Canadian desk. And with more than half of our trades coming from non-Canadian clients (U.S. and Europe), we have a much more natural product to show our clients than the Canadian domestic dealers.

**Q.  So what do you look for when hiring potential traders?**

A.  I look for candidates that show initiative. The individual has to be a team player and a self-starter. These are important characteristics. They must also be willing to do the menial jobs (like we all do) in order to make the desk successful. Having said that, I want this person to have enough drive to want my job.

### Profile of the Ideal Institutional Equity Trader

The ideal institutional equity trader should have the following attributes:

- street smarts
- ability to think on one's feet
- market savvy
- ability to handle and work under pressure
- a strong sense of urgency
- the ability to multi-task
- tenacity and aggressiveness
- integrity
- selling skills
- strong interpersonal skills
- good memory
- personable—the ability to build and maintain strong client relationships
- an excellent customer service ethic
- good product knowledge
- team player
- knowledge of the stocks' fundamentals
- an interest and understanding of financial markets

## The 10 Largest Institutional Equity Sales Teams in Canada*

| Company | Number of Team Members |
|---|---|
| 1. RBC Capital Markets | 24 |
| 2. BMO NesbittBurns | 23 |
| 3. CIBC World Markets | 22 |
| 4. TD Newcrest | 22 |
| 5. Scotia Capital | 20 |
| 6. UBS Securities Canada | 19 |
| 7. National Bank Financial | 16 |
| 8. GMP Securities | 15 |
| 9. Merrill Lynch Canada | 13 |
| 10. Canaccord Capital | 12 |

\* Measured by number of agency and liability traders based in North America trading Canadian and/or interlisted stocks.

## Suggested Reading

1. *Against the Gods: The Remarkable Story of Risk* (by Peter L. Bernstein, published by John Wiley & Sons Canada)

   This business best-seller presents a historical study of risk and the evolution of risk management, and the use of probability theory in the financial markets.

2. *An Introduction to Technical Analysis* (Reuters Financial Training Series) (by Reuters, published by John Wiley & Sons)

An overview of technical analysis intended for the novice student of the markets.

3. *Competitive Strategy: Techniques for Analyzing Industries and Competitors* (by Michael E. Porter, published by Free Press)

   Considered the Old Testament on business strategy, Michael E. Porter (a Harvard Business School professor) provides a disciplined framework for understanding the fundamentals of business competition.

4. *Fooled by Randomness: The Hidden Role of Chance in the Markets and in Life* (by Nassim Nicholas Taleb, published by Texere Publishing)

   Written by a former options trader who now runs a hedge fund, this book explores the role of probability and unforeseen events in the market.

5. *Intermarket Analysis: Profiting from Global Market Relationships* (by John Murphy, published by John Wiley & Sons)

   Written by the guru of technical analysis, this book provides insights into how the stock, bond, currency, and commodity markets are linked together.

6. *Liar's Poker: Rising Through the Wreckage on Wall Street* (by Michael Leweis, published by W.W. Norton & Co.)

   A fascinating personal memoir of the author's four years with Salomon Brothers as a bond trader during the go-go years of the late 1980s.

7. *Market Wizards: Interviews with Top Traders* (by Jack D. Schwager, published by HarperBusiness)

This best-selling business classic is the original in the Market Wizards series. It includes trading philosophies and lessons by some of the top traders across the spectrum of financial markets.

8. *Martin Pring's Introduction to Technical Analysis: A CD-ROM Seminar and Workbook* (by Martin J. Pring, published by McGraw-Hill)

A good interactive tutorial for those getting started in technical analysis.

9. *The New Market Wizards: Conversations with America's Top Traders* (by Jack D. Schwager, published by HarperBusiness)

More trading insights from some of the most successful traders.

10. *Reminiscences of a Stock Operator* (by Edwin Lefèvre and Marketplace Books, published by John Wiley & Sons)

Considered a must-read among professional traders. Just about every trader I spoke to recommended this book.

11. *Stan Weinstein's Secrets for Profiting in Bull and Bear Markets* (by Stan Weinstein, published by Irwin Professional Publishing)

An introductory text on technical analysis, this book doesn't present any math or formulas but instead discusses the use of price, volume, and trend data to forecast stock movements.

12. *Stock Market Logic* (by Norman Fosback, published by Dearborn Trade Publishing)

After having gone through 18 printings, this book is now out of print so it is hard to come by. Some well-regarded technical analysts consider it something of a classic.

13. *Stock Market Wizards: Interviews with America's Top Stock Traders* (by Jack D. Schwager, published by HarperBusiness)

Another set of Q&A sessions with some of the best stock traders.

14. *Technical Analysis from A to Z* (by Steven B. Achelis, published by McGraw-Hill Trade)

A good reference book for those looking for an overview of the basic principles of technical analysis. Summaries on more than 100 technical indicators are presented.

15. *Technical Analysis of the Financial Markets: A Comprehensive Guide to Trading Methods and Applications* (by John J. Murphy, published by Prentice Hall)

The author (former director of Merrill Lynch's Technical Analysis Futures Division and technical analysis commentator for CNBC) of best-seller *Technical Analysis of the Futures Markets* presents this updated and expanded edition to include all of the financial markets. This text provides a more in-depth treatment of the subject of technical analysis and is therefore better suited to readers with more than a basic understanding of the subject.

16. *The Traders: Inside Canada's Stock Markets* (by Alexander Ross, published by Collins)

Published two decades ago, award-winning business writer Alexander Ross gives us insights into the subculture of the Canadian investment industry that existed then and the history and backgrounds of the players that are still in the game today.

CHAPTER

Investment
**BANKER**

# Investment Banker

## Overview

INVESTMENT BANKING (IBK) is a high-pressure, demanding job with brutal hours, and can involve working with some difficult personalities. But the opportunity to work on high-profile transactions with some extremely bright professionals and earn a much-better-than-average living can make it all worthwhile. Furthermore, after spending time in a corporate finance role, one learns how a company works, hones financial skills and company valuation techniques, develops business judgment, and acquires capital markets experience. The skills learned here will serve as the foundation to any business career.

Investment banking is typically composed of three areas:

1. corporate finance: the process of raising debt and equity capital for corporations

2. public finance: the process of raising capital for governments and government agencies

3. mergers & acquisitions: the process of providing strategic advisory services on mergers, acquisitions, asset divestitures and corporate restructurings, valuations, and fairness opinions

**QUICK FACTS**

**EDUCATION**
Undergraduate and/or
graduate degree in
finance/economics or law

**COMPENSATION RANGE**
$75,000 – $1.5 million

**INDUSTRY CERTIFICATION**
CFA designation recommended

For the purposes of this chapter, the majority of comments are focused on corporate finance and, more specifically, on the equity underwriting business. Equity underwriting (as opposed to debt underwriting) is the most profitable part of the business but it is highly correlated to market and sector performance. Therefore, the investment banking business is a cyclical one. In a robust market, IPOs get priced at the high end of the target range, more of these shares are sold than anticipated (and brokers exercise the "greenshoe"), and the stock trades above issue price. In a soft market, the opposite happens and IPOs/financings regularly get shelved. Therefore, I-banking jobs have the highest betas on the wholesale side of the business relative to research, sales, and trading. In a bull market, you're working 100-hour weeks and making good bonuses (but you can kiss your personal life goodbye). In bear markets, a brokerage firm's cost-cutting efforts are most noticeable in the ranks of I-bankers, so these jobs are often the first to go.

As one moves up the pecking order in the I-banking world, there is more client interaction and more responsibility to build and maintain corporate client relationships. Regardless of the exact titles, there are essentially three levels in the IBK group: the junior bankers are the *analysts* and the *associates*, the relationship managers are the *vice presidents/associate directors* and the *directors/executive directors*, and the senior managers/rainmakers are the *managing directors*. Put more succinctly, the grinders, the minders, and the finders.

### Education

Investment banking analysts are hired straight out of undergraduate business/economics programs to do the number-crunching (the grunt work) for their department. After two years on the job, most I-banking analysts go to graduate school to do an MBA or LLB, or a combined degree. A few analysts, however, are invited to stay on for a third year as an analyst and are then fast-tracked into an associate role in the fourth year.

### Compensation Range

Investment banking is the one area where being a managing director (at a tier one dealer) means that you're on track to make seven figures. Getting there is at least a decade-long journey, though. After spending a couple of years as an I-banking analyst and then going to graduate school, it's still another nine years before making it to the managing director level. (The rule of thumb in terms of progression through the I-banking ranks is "3-3-3"—three years as an associate, then three years as a vice president/associate director, then three years as a director/executive director.)

Following are the approximate annual compensation (salary plus bonus) ranges for the various I-banking levels at the domestic bank-owned firms:

Director/executive director: $500,000–$750,000

Vice president/associate director: $250,000–$500,000

Associate: $150,000–$250,000

Analyst: $75,000–$150,000

There are a number of factors that determine individual compensation:

- **Equity deal volumes.** The volume of equity transactions and the resulting profitability of brokerage firms are the prime determinants of industry compensation levels (and employment levels).

- **The number of deals led.** The lead underwriter on a deal gets the largest share of the transaction fees.

- **The industry sector.** An I-banker working in a "hot" sector—one where investor interest is driving up the stock values, trading volumes, and investment banking business—will likely get a better bonus than one working in a sector where there is little or no investor interest.

- **Personal performance.** Just work hard, deliver more than is asked for, and hope for the best.

- **Seniority.** All things being equal, professionals at any given level can expect a better bonus in year two and even better in year three.

- **The type of firm.** Global and U.S. dealers tend to pay at the higher end of the range.

- **Street/market value.** The current market value of a competitor is always useful as an indicator.

### Industry Certification

Having the CFA designation is highly recommended. The CFA designation has become the standard in the investment/finance industry. The program may or may not make you a better dealmaker but successful completion of the program has become a rite of passage into the institutional investment community. When one looks around the community, most professionals have the designation so having it doesn't set you apart—but not having it will.

To earn the CFA charter, a CFA candidate must pass three six-hour examinations (CFA Institute recommends that 250 hours of study is needed to prepare for each exam) and have spent three years working in a role where he or she is involved in the investment decision-making process.

The average pass rate for each level of the exams tends to hover around 50%. Of the approximately 56,000 CFA charterholders worldwide, only a few have passed all three exams consecutively.

## Getting Started

The most common source of recruits for investment banking *analyst* positions are the campus recruiting efforts aimed at undergraduate business/economics programs.

Campus recruiting is the annual ritual whereby the major brokerage firms visit select universities across Canada—typically between mid-September and the end of October—to hire for the following spring. The 2-hour information sessions consist of 30-40 minute company presentations and then allow time for the students to mingle with company representatives. Although the investment banks tend to target MBA students, undergraduate commerce students are sometimes invited to participate.

The process is highly competitive. Each investment bank will do their rounds to 6-8 universities across Canada and may only be looking to fill two spots.

The process starts in early September when the investment banks post advertisements for the positions they're looking to fill. At the information sessions, students have an opportunity to ask questions about the jobs. Students interested in applying for the jobs will hand their résumés to the career/placement office. The placement office submits the résumés to the company who then determines a short list of candidates they want to interview. The placement office is advised of the short list and contacts the students to arrange the first round of interviews, which typically take place on campus. Of the students selected for the first round, less than half progress to round two. The second round of interviews is called Super Saturdays where students from across the country participate in a number of back-to-back interviews at the company's head offices.

The most common sources of recruits for investment banking *associate* positions are:

• the campus recruiting aimed at graduate business/economics/law programs

- promotions from analyst ranks

- legal firms (corporate/securities law)

- accounting firms

- equity research associates

Furthermore, having one or more of the following experiences should help you get your first job as an I-banking analyst or associate:

- **Summer internships.** Several firms offer summer internship programs in their investment banking group.

- **University co-op programs.** A number of undergraduate business programs offer co-op work terms where select students are placed with participating employers in the business community.

- **University investment programs.** Several universities (University of British Columbia, University of Calgary, University of New Brunswick, and Concordia University) offer a program where a select group of (typically eight) commerce students manages a portfolio of securities, participates in lectures by mentors (Bay Street professionals), and is placed in summer positions with participating investment dealers and money management firms.

Once you land an analyst or associate role, you will likely be assigned to an industry subgroup. Industry subgroups specialize along industry lines (e.g., financial institutions, healthcare, etc.), while product groups specialize by type of investment vehicle (e.g., investment grade debt). At several of the larger investment dealers, junior I-bankers are expected to do at least one industry group rotation before moving on to the relationship management level.

If you're serious about landing a job in investment banking, it will be useful to start by familiarizing yourself with some of the terminology, and understanding the deal process. What follows are the more relevant I-banking terms, a brief discussion of a bought deal versus a marketed deal, and a graph showing the evolution of a marketed deal.

### Relevant Investment Banking Terminology

Bonus credit formula: a methodology used for the purposes of determining the rankings of dealers in the underwriting league tables, where the bookrunner is credited with two shares of the transaction and the rest of the syndicate members each receive one share. See **bookrunner** and **underwriting league tables**.

Bookrunner: a term used to define the lead/key role played by one or more dealers on a financing; typically the lead underwriter(s).

Bought deal: a form of equity financing pioneered in Canada whereby the underwriter (or group of underwriters) uses the firm's own capital to buy the whole issue and then immediately resells the stock to institutional and retail clients.

Full credit formula: a methodology used for the purposes of determining the rankings of dealers in the underwriting league tables, where the lead underwriter receives credit for the whole transaction. See **underwriting league tables**.

Fully marketed deal: a form of financing in which the underwriter (or group of underwriters) acts as an agent for the issuer and actively markets the management team and its story to institutional and retail clients.

Greensheet: a document used by the syndicate as a marketing tool that provides a summary of the offering, an overview of the issuing company, and investment highlights; formally known as a Confidential Information Memorandum.

Greenshoe: an overallotment option whereby the underwriters can sell additional (usually 15% more) stock if there is excess demand of an issue.

Initial public offering (IPO): the act of taking companies public by selling stock to the public for the first time.

Issuer: the corporate client that issues securities (stocks or bonds) to raise money.

Jump-ball economics: also known as *incentive economics*, this system of allocating commissions to the underwriters of a transaction gives fund managers the power to determine which underwriters get how much commission. Under the conventional system, the issuer and its investment bankers sit down ahead of time and carve up the commission pie, and regardless of how much work a firm does on the deal, the commission payout remains fixed. Under jump-ball economics, the bookrunner tends to get a disproportionately large percentage of the fees.

Offering memorandum: a document outlining the details of a private placement of securities; on the other hand, a securities issue offered for sale to the public requires the preparation and filing of a formal prospectus. See **prospectus**.

Private placement: an issue of securities sold to a limited group of investors (typically institutions and high-net-worth individuals).

Prospectus: a document prepared by the lead underwriter and processed/approved by the applicable securities commissions outlining the details of the securities being offered for sale to the public.

Road show: during a fully marketed equity deal, the process where the lead underwriter markets the company's senior management team to institutional and retail investors to present the merits of the company/deal. See **fully marketed deal**.

Secondary offering: a subsequent or follow-on offering of securities after the company has gone public.

Short form prospectus: an abbreviated version of the prospectus that can be used prior to a securities issue by certain issuers—those with prompt offering prospectus (POP) status. "POP" issuers who meet the eligibility requirements (e.g., have been a reporting issuer for at least a year, have a market capitalization of at least $75 million, etc.) are allowed to issue freely trading stock but cannot pre-market their securities issue.

Syndicate: a group of brokerage houses that act together to underwrite and sell a particular equity (or debt) issue.

Underwriting fees: fees earned by a brokerage firm for underwriting a deal. The fee is influenced by two main factors: the size of the deal (generally, the larger the deal, the lower the percentage) and whether the deal is an initial public offering (the fee for an IPO tends to be higher to compensate for the extra work involved relative to a follow-on financing). In Canada, fees earned by the underwriters typically range from 4% to 6.5% of the deal size. In the United States, the fee ranges from 2.5% to 7%.

Underwriting league tables: the annual rankings of investment dealers by the gross proceeds (total value of money raised) of the deals they underwrote; the rankings are typically categorized by *type* of financing (e.g., equity, debt, IPOs, etc.).

### Bought Deal Versus Fully Marketed Deal

As defined earlier, a bought deal is a form of equity financing pioneered in Canada whereby the underwriter (or group of underwriters) uses the firm's own capital to buy the whole issue and then immediately resells the stock to institutional and retail clients. A fully marketed deal, on the other hand, is a form of financing in which the underwriter (or group of underwriters) acts as an agent for the issuer and actively markets the management team and its story to institutional and retail clients.


### Bought Deal

For follow-on common share financings, the majority of deals (up to 80%, as suggested by industry participants) are bought deals.

Advantages to corporate issuer:

- Expeditious way to raise capital. A bought deal takes very little of management's time because no marketing or road shows are involved.

- Lower cost. Investment banking fees are usually less for bought deals than for fully marketed deals.

Advantage to investment dealer:

- Quick way to raise capital for corporate clients. It takes less of investment dealers' time to do a bought deal than to do a fully marketed deal because no marketing or road shows are involved.

Advantage to buyer of the stock:

- Provides liquidity to institutional clients in that they can buy large positions in companies with minimal movement in the stock's price. This is because the announcement of a fully marketed equity deal tends to knock the stock back due to the dilution effects on current shareholders.


### Fully Marketed Deal

In Canada, all initial public offerings are fully marketed deals. Only approximately 20% of follow-on financings are fully-marketed.

# EVOLUTION OF A MARKETED DEAL

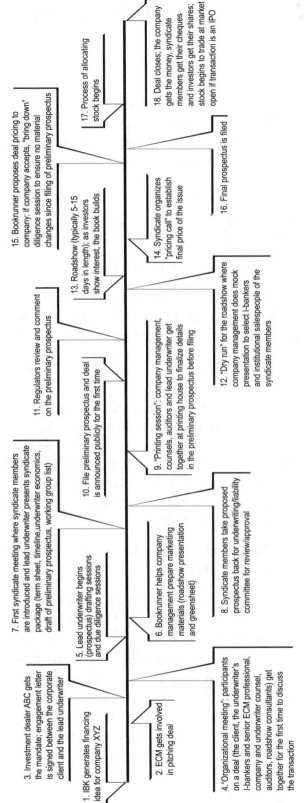

1. IBK generates financing idea for company XYZ

2. ECM gets involved in pitching deal

3. Investment dealer ABC gets the mandate; engagement letter is signed between the corporate client and the lead underwriter

4. "Organizational meeting": participants on a deal (the client, the underwriter's I-bankers and senior ECM professional, company and underwriter counsel, auditors, roadshow consultants) get together for the first time to discuss the transaction

5. Lead underwriter begins (prospectus) drafting sessions and due diligence sessions

6. Bookrunner helps company management prepare marketing materials (roadshow presentation and greensheet)

7. First syndicate meeting where syndicate members are introduced and lead underwriter presents syndicate package (term sheet, timeline, underwriter economics, draft of preliminary prospectus, working group list)

8. Syndicate members take proposed prospectus back for underwriting/liability committee for review/approval

9. "Printing session": company management, counsels, auditors and lead underwriter get together at printing house to finalize details in the preliminary prospectus before filing

10. File preliminary prospectus and deal is announced publicly for the first time

11. Regulators review and comment on the preliminary prospectus

12. "Dry run" for the roadshow where company management does mock presentation to select I-bankers and institutional salespeople of the syndicate members

13. Roadshow (typically 5-15 days in length); as investors show interest, the book builds

14. Syndicate organizes "pricing call" to establish final price of the issue

15. Bookrunner proposes deal pricing to company; if company accepts, "bring down" diligence session to ensure no material changes since filing of preliminary prospectus

16. Final prospectus is filed

17. Process of allocating stock begins

18. Deal closes; the company gets the money, syndicate members get their cheques and investors get their shares; stock begins to trade at market open if transaction is an IPO

Source: Kan & Associates Inc.

Advantage to corporate issuer:

- Publicity. Marketing efforts undertaken during a fully marketed deal allow management the opportunity to tell its story to the Street and possibly increase the institutional shareholder base.

Advantage to investment dealer:

- Much lower risk to the underwriters. The capital of the dealer is not at risk as it is in a bought deal transaction.

Advantage to buyer of the stock:

- The ability to do due diligence. Institutional clients prefer fully marketed deals because they have an opportunity to meet company management and do their due diligence.

## A Day in the Life of a
## Top Investment Banking Associate

**Aaron Lau** is an investment banking associate in the North American Industrials Group of TD Securities. Mr. Lau is an alumnus of the highly regarded University of British Columbia Portfolio Management Foundation program.

Bachelor of Commerce (Honours) from University of British Columbia, 2001

I began to pursue a career in finance early in my university education. My first foray into the industry came at the hands of two investment advisors at BMO Nesbitt Burns who offered me a part-time role during my second year. There, I had my first opportunity to be on the front lines and to learn about the capital markets and how to cold call. This job ultimately led to my acceptance in the Portfolio Management Foundation (PMF) program, a two-year extracurricular program in which a select group of students is given the opportunity to manage a balanced portfolio of $2.7 million, take part in two summers of internships and have tremendous access to an extensive network of mentors and alumni on both the buy-side and sell-side of the Street. This program was and continues to be instrumental in my career development.

My internships in the PMF program consisted of two summers in the equity research departments of CIBC World Markets and Goepel McDermid (now Raymond James), where I had the opportunity to work with top-ranked analysts to sharpen my financial modelling, research, and writing skills. As well, the internships provided me with my first glimpse of investment banking. After much research, I decided to pursue a career in investment banking for the following reasons: one, it utilized the same skill set I developed during my equity research summers; two, the job was fast-paced and offered clear promotional opportunities; and three, compensation was on the high end of entry-level positions on Bay Street.

Once recruiting season began, I interviewed with most major North American investment dealers and ultimately began my career with Credit Suisse First Boston. Fast-forward three years, and after much time spent putting together pitch books and financial models, I've had the good fortune to be involved in some significant transactions. Today, I am part of a high-intensity team of investment banking professionals at TD Securities who focus specifically on the North American industrials sector. Our aim is to provide our clients with high-quality advice and timely execution in the areas of financing and strategic advisory services. At the analyst and associate level, this generally comes in the form of being able to craft our ideas into a concise and cogent pitch book.

For the uninitiated, the road to securing an associate position is a graduated process. The most conventional methods on the Street are via a direct promotion after three years as an analyst or through MBA school. The latter is particularly true for some-one wishing to break into the industry for the first time. I find that either approach is invariably tied to the state of the markets. During the Internet boom, financial institutions were losing talent to start-up firms and, as a result, were quick to allow more direct promotions. On the other hand, in tough markets and with plenty of talent to choose from, firms may decide that a business school candidate is more preferable. The general state of the Street today remains mixed. Some firms continue to offer direct promotion opportunities, whereas others will only consider MBA graduates.

The life of an associate is a pleasure to describe. In a sentence, the job is demanding, can be monoto-nous at times, requires plenty of sacrifices, but is always rewarding in one form or another. The hours vary from 70 to 100 hours per week. I find that the role of the associate often draws parallels from both the analyst and vice president levels. For example, processing pitch books and working on complex financial models remain the core duties of any associ-ate. This is balanced, however, by a certain level of client interaction, deal processing, and idea genera-tion opportunities.

Everyday is different for an associate as the job constantly evolves around projects and deals. For instance, during quiet times, the team may spend an inordinate amount of time generating M&A ideas for a client and subsequently putting together detailed analyses concerning the target company, strategic rationale, and pro forma financial impact of a potential acquisition. When a live deal (meaning the firm is mandated to lead the transaction) hits, however, an associate staffed on the deal will be unable to afford time on other projects.

In my opinion, the two most rewarding moments in being an associate are being able to sit with CEOs and CFOs of a public company to discuss financing and advisory ideas, and being able to work on a live deal from start to finish and reading about it in the newspaper the next day. This is what inevitably gets me up in the morning and keeps me awake during the late nights.

A typical day as an investment banking associate might look like this:

**8:00 a.m.**  Arrive at work, check voicemails, and scan newspapers and websites for any news items of interest.

**8:15 a.m.**  Managing director (MD) gets the team together to see what projects we have on the go and which clients we are meeting this week.

**8:30 a.m.**  Resume work on an M&A pitch for company XYZ due tomorrow. Spend the next hour reviewing the book with the director and scrubbing the financial models with the analyst.

**9:30 a.m.**  Prepare to head out with the MD and the head of equity capital markets (ECM) to meet with a client regarding equity financing opportunities.

**11:00 a.m.**  Meeting results in some follow-up work, which we will revisit later this week.

**11:30 a.m.**  Arrive back at the office and check voicemails. Review the latest draft of the M&A pitch. After some adjustments and tweaking, I provide the director with another turn of the book.

**1:00 p.m.**    Pick up a quick lunch at the food court.

**1:20 p.m.**    MD pulls me into his office and lets me know of an upcoming meeting two days from now. Company ABC wants to chat about debt financing. The team would like to see a good draft of the presentation first thing tomorrow morning.

**1:30 p.m.**    Begin scrambling to put a book together on what we need for company ABC. The analyst takes on the "comps" (comparable-company analyses) while I start looking after other sections of the book.

**3:00 p.m.**    MD wants to add another acquisition target to the M&A pitch for company XYZ. The analyst and I begin tag-teaming to make the necessary additions to the book.

**5:00 p.m.**    Updates to the M&A pitch are done. One final draft goes around and the director and other team members sign-off on the M&A pitch for company XYZ.

**6:00 p.m.**    The book for company XYZ goes to print for tomorrow's meeting. I begin to go over briefing materials and study the financial data in the pitch in the event questions arise during the meeting.

**6:45 p.m.**    Hunger strikes and the analyst is kind enough to pick up dinner for the team. It's sushi night.

**7:15 p.m.**    Back to working on the debt financing pitch. I review the comps with the analyst and make some adjustments and additions to the calculations. Time to put other sections of the book together and to conduct extensive analysis on the various alternatives and cost impact of debt financing strategies for company ABC.

**9:30 p.m.**    The draft for company ABC is in good shape. Time to dig through the inbox and finish up some ongoing work from last week.

**10:15 p.m.**    Call it a night.

# HOW INVESTMENT BANKING ANALYSTS SPEND THEIR TIME

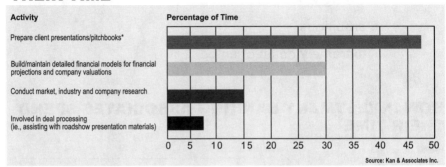

| Activity | Percentage of Time |
|---|---|
| Prepare client presentations/pitchbooks* | |
| Build/maintain detailed financial models for financial projections and company valuations | |
| Conduct market, industry and company research | |
| Involved in deal processing (ie., assisting with roadshow presentation materials) | |

Source: Kan & Associates Inc.

\* Essentially a business development presentation that a) promotes the firm's underwriting, research and trading capabilities, and b) presents a proposed corporate finance transaction (financing proposal, new issue idea, etc.)

The above percentages tend to change depending on:

- **Deal flow.** When the IBK group has several deals that are live, the focus is on executing those transactions, so naturally more time is spent on preparing the road show/marketing materials, assisting with the documentation, doing due diligence, etc.

### Profile of the Ideal Investment Banking *Analyst* Candidate

From a senior investment banker's perspective, the ideal IBK analyst should meet the following criteria:

- undergraduate degree from a respected university
- a history of exceptional academic achievement
- strong financial modelling and quantitative skills
- strong research and analytical skills
- excellent communication skills (both verbal and written)
- self-starter

- ability to perform under pressure

- strong work ethic

- ambitious

- extremely detail-oriented

## HOW INVESTMENT BANKING ASSOCIATES SPEND THEIR TIME

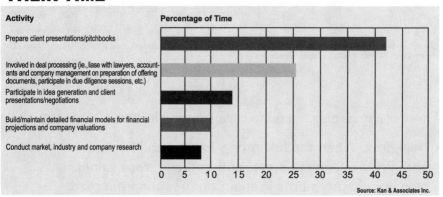

Source: Kan & Associates Inc.

The above percentages tend to change depending on:

- **Deal flow.** When the IBK group has several deals that are live, the focus is on deal processing.

- **Whether the associate's firm is the bookrunner.** The responsibility of executing/processing a transaction rests with the bookrunner, therefore the bookrunner's associates are the ones liaising with lawyers, accountants, and company management regarding the preparation of offering documents, participating in due diligence sessions, etc.

- **Seniority of the associate.** The senior associates get more responsibility for idea generation and client presentations/negotiations than do junior associates.

### Profile of the Ideal Investment
### Banking *Associate* Candidate

From a senior investment banker's perspective, the ideal IBK associate should meet the following criteria:

- MBA/LLB and/or CFA

- relevant work experience

- a history of exceptional academic achievement

- strong financial modelling and quantitative skills

- strong research and analytical skills

- excellent communication skills (both verbal and written)

- self-starter

- ability to perform under pressure

- strong work ethic

- ambitious

- extremely detail-oriented

- a developing ability to interact with clients

## A Chat with a Head of Investment Banking

**Pat Meneley**, vice-chair at TD Securities, is head of the firm's investment banking division. He was previously a vice president with Salomon Smith Barney Canada (now Citigroup Global Markets). Mr. Meneley was a 2002 recipient of the "Canada's Top 40 Under 40" award.

**Q. How did you get your start in the business?**

A.  I started as an I-banking associate at TD Securities after completing my MBA at the University of Western Ontario. After a year on the job, Salomon Smith Barney approached me. While the opportunity at TD Securities was a very good one, the Salomon opportunity offered several interesting aspects: the best associate training program on Wall Street, the chance to work in New York City, and the experience of working with a U.S. bulge bracket dealer. I returned to TD Securities six years later to run the Communications & Media Group, and became Head of Investment Banking three years after that.

**Q.  What experiences helped shape your IBK career?**

A.  Both my academic and early work experiences were instrumental in shaping my career. The undergraduate business program at the University of British Columbia (UBC) was highly quantitative, with excellent, top-quality faculty that pushed us hard and made us push ourselves, and where the professors were writing leading-edge articles in respected industry publications like the *Journal of Finance*. Then I entered the graduate business program at University of Western Ontario (UWO) Richard Ivey School of Business. It was well-recognized for its case-study approach, which emphasized the application of concepts, and an interactive learning environment—it was a nice complement to the UBC program. In terms of work experiences, the Salomon associate training program in New York City (a rigorous 10-week program with about 40 associates from around the world) was perhaps the best grounding that I could have received in this business. Furthermore, I've had the benefit of working for, and alongside, some exceptionally talented professionals who've achieved some great things. My mentors at Salomon Smith Barney were great role models because they demonstrated how to achieve balance in life. Balance doesn't mean no intensity and it doesn't mean no commitment—it means always learning, it means having a strong desire to win; it means maintaining a level of intensity and not wasting a single minute of the day, and at the same time having a commitment to family life and raising happy, successful children with good values.

**Q. Which of your (business) philosophies has contributed to your success?**

A. I think my emphasis on certain personal characteristics like integrity, common sense, a strong work ethic, and being passionate about everything I do has been instrumental in getting me where I am today. To me, those are fundamental values and you can't do anything well without them.

In our business—which is a service business—you have to put the client first and really understand what the client is trying to achieve. Then you come up with a solution that is tailored to address their objectives more effectively than your competitors' solutions.

I also believe that one should get involved in the community in a meaningful way because it's important to give something back and make an impact. And by giving back, I don't mean simply making financial contributions (charity fundraising efforts) but giving time and intellect (volunteer work). It's only right that we lend a hand to people less fortunate than ourselves because not everyone has been given the opportunities that some of us here on Bay Street have been given. And here I want to give an example of being passionate about the things we do. Here at TD, I've tried to instill a culture of giving, and I see passion and the culture of giving come together as we compete with the other investment dealers not only on deals but on charity giving as well.

**Q. TD Securities' investment banking group is consistently in the top five of equity underwriters in the country. What do you credit that to?**

A. We have strong people in every part of our wholesale business—investment banking, equity capital markets, research, and sales/trading. Strength in *all* areas is crucial for the group to consistently win. When you have a good, balanced team that matches clients' objectives with market opportunities, it results in great execution.

**Q.   The common wisdom is that the following factors determine which investment firm wins the deal(s): credit facilities/lending capabilities, retail distribution, research, sales/trading. Would you agree?**

A.   I believe that those elements are important tools in terms of building relationships with corporate issuers but I think there are other reasons why an underwriter may win the business of any given client. In broader terms, I think having a reputation for being able to do fair deals is very important. A fair deal is one in which both the corporate issuer—the seller of securities—and the institutional client—the buyer of the securities—feel that it was a good transaction. More specifically, the factors I believe determine which investment firm wins any given deal are:

- The ability to price deals appropriately in the context of the market. This is where having strong people in all parts of the wholesale business comes to bear. You need the key professionals from IBK, ECM, research, and sales/trading all delivering essential information into the pricing of a deal to have a good feel for, and understanding of, the market.

- Relationships between the issuer and the underwriter. The corporate client must trust the underwriter's ability to deliver.

- Commitment of resources. The issuer must also know that the underwriter will commit its best people to that client's file/transaction.

**Q.   What is the biggest misconception about the IBK job?**

A.   I think there's a few young recruits that see the glamorous side of the job—being on planes, and doing pitches to

senior-level management on headline-grabbing transactions. But the reality is that they're likely to be flying back on
the red-eye flight after working several 17-hour days in a
row and will have to go straight into the office in the morning. So it's actually a lot of hard work, but it's lots of fun (and
very lucrative) when you win in this business.

**Q. In what ways has the new regulatory environment
changed the day-to-day life of an I-banker?**

A.  The new regulatory environment primarily affects the
research analysts. Here at TD, we've historically had a high
awareness of regulatory and ethical issues so we've
always had the appropriate level of separation between
research and investment banking. We are fully compliant.
In fact, I am personally involved in ensuring that all TDSI
investment banking staff maintain the integrity of our
department and the firm.

**Q. What do you look for when hiring a junior investment
banker?**

A.  In terms of credentials, we like to hire young professionals
into our associate program who have an MBA, CA, or CFA.
I also look for several personal attributes/characteristics:

- Intelligence. By intelligence I don't mean just book
  smarts and good grades but having good instincts.

- Track record of achievement. We look at both academic
  and extracurricular activities to try and spot talent. We
  want the candidates who we think are going to be winners.

- Commitment/work ethic. We want passionate hard workers.

- "Fit" factor. By fit, I don't mean just personality-wise. We
  like to hire candidates that will fit into our culture and that
  share our values.

**Q.  What advice would you give to a young I-banker?**

**A.  To be honest, I don't give much advice—I lead by example.**

"Try to build a good relationship with the institutional sales desk and buy-side clients as well as the corporate clients. The best way to maintain, and enhance, these relationships is to bring quality deals to the table that are priced so both sets of clients can make money. Not every deal will make money but as long as more make money than lose money, then you build repeat business and a personal franchise for the long term."

*—Ali Bhojani, Senior Investment Banker, Dundee Securities*

## Comparing an Investment Banker with a Corporate Banker

|  | Investment Banker | Corporate Banker |
|---|---|---|
| Hours worked per week | 80–100 | 40–50 |
| Focus of financial analysis | Income statement-driven to assess earnings potential | Cash flow-driven to assess credit risk |
| Service provided | Raising capital by selling equity or debt securities | Facilitating loans |
| Account management | Maintain investor interest in the securities they underwrite | Monitor covenant compliance |

| Contribution to firm profitability | High margins | Thin margins |
|---|---|---|

## 2003's Top Equity Dealmakers in Canada

| Underwriter | Total Number | Total Amount (in Millions of Dollars) |
|---|---|---|
| 1. CIBC World Markets | 115 | 12,910 |
| 2. RBC Capital Markets | 58 | 6,292 |
| 3. Scotia Capital | 56 | 5,407 |
| 4. BMO Nesbitt Burns | 52 | 3,599 |
| 5. TD Securities | 30 | 2,160 |
| 6. Merrill Lynch Canada | 8 | 1,521 |
| 7. National Bank Financial | 27 | 1,460 |
| 8. UBS Securities Canada | 5 | 1,272 |
| 9. GMP Securities | 66 | 1,254 |
| 10. Canaccord Capital | 103 | 1,053 |
| 11. Citigroup Global Markets | 5 | 842 |
| 12. Orion Securities | 36 | 510 |
| 13. Morgan Stanley & Co. | 3 | 421 |
| 14. Dundee Securities | 34 | 323 |
| 15. Haywood Securities | 43 | 304 |
| 16. FirstEnergy Capital | 28 | 303 |
| 17. Banc of America Securities | 2 | 296 |
| 18. Peters & Co. | 16 | 285 |
| 19. Sprott Securities | 12 | 273 |
| 20. Raymond James | 19 | 247 |

Source: *National Post*

## Suggested Reading

1. *Applied Corporate Finance: A User's Manual* (by Aswath Damodaran, published by John Wiley & Sons)

   Written by an NYU Stern Business School finance professor, this text focuses on converting financial theory into practical financial analysis.

2. *The Art of M&A: A Merger Acquisition Buyout Guide* (by Stanley Foster Reed, et al., published by McGraw-Hill)

   This practical reference book is fairly comprehensive, from the methods in selecting, valuing, and financing candidates/targets for acquisition to what to do when you are a target of an acquisition.

3. *Barbarians at the Gate* (by Bryan Burrough and John Helyar, published by Harper Business)

   A business book classic, this narrative of the leveraged buyout of RJR Nabisco Corp. for $25 billion underscores the greed and excesses of the '80s.

4. *Bigwig Briefs: Become an Investment Banker: The Real World Intelligence Necessary to Become a Successful Investment Banker* (by Aspatore Books Staff, published by Aspatore Books)

   Interviews with 10 "bigwigs" (six investment bankers and four venture capitalists). The book doesn't give any advice on becoming an investment banker but does give some insight into what investment bankers do.

5. *The Business of Investment Banking* (by K. Thomas Liaw, published by John Wiley & Sons)

This is a good overview of the investment banking business and the key trends affecting the future of the business.

6. *Corporate Finance: A Valuation Approach* (by Simon Z. Benninga and Oded Sarig, published by McGraw– Hill/Irwin)

   This text provides a good introduction into the valuation of assets, companies, and individual securities. It provides step-by-step guidance toward company valuation and building financial models.

7. *Damodaran on Valuation: Security Analysis for Investment and Corporate Finance* (by Aswath Damodaran, published by John Wiley & Sons)

   The NYU Stern Business School finance professor provides a good overview of three valuation approaches for investment analysis: discounted cash flow, relative valuation, and contingent claim valuation.

8. *Doing Deals: Investment Banks at Work* (by Robert G. Eccles and Dwight B. Crane, published by Harvard Business School Press)

   Executives from several major Wall Street investment banks reveal their firms' management practices. Although slightly dated, one can still glean some insights into the structure of the industry, how bonuses are determined, relationship management issues, etc.

9. *Financial Modeling—2nd Edition* (by Simon Benninga and Benjamin Czaczkes, published by MIT Press)

   This is a good book on the fundamentals of spreadsheet modelling using Excel.

10. *Handbook of Canadian Security Analysis, Volumes I & II* (edited by Joe Kan, published by John Wiley & Sons)

   This valuable reference is a guide to evaluating the industry sectors of the market. Some 28 of Canada's top-ranked sell-side analysts were hand-picked to share their expertise and experience in understanding and analyzing the fundamental forces that drive stock performance in each industry group.

11. *Harvard Business Review on Mergers & Acquisitions* (by Dennis Carey, et al., published by Harvard Business Book Press)

   A collection of articles from leading business scholars. Topics covered include the early planning and valuing of acquisition targets through to the post-merger integration issues.

12. *Investment Valuation: Tools and Techniques for Determining the Value of Any Asset* (by Aswath Damodaran, published by John Wiley & Sons)

   Another book by the NYU finance professor, this is a comprehensive guide for determining the value of both financial assets (stocks, bonds, options, futures) and real assets (real estate).

13. *M&A: A Practical Guide to Doing the Deal* (by Jeffrey C. Hooke, published by John Wiley & Sons)

   This text gives its target audience (corporate executives and junior investment professionals) an understanding of basic deal concepts and an overview of the mergers & acquisitions process.

14. *Masters of the Universe: Winning Strategies of America's Greatest Deal Makers* (by Daniel J. Kadlec, published by Harper Business)

*Time* magazine's Wall Street columnist profiles nine of the biggest dealmakers of our era and the most important, headline-grabbing deal of each's career.

15. *Monkey Business: Swinging Through the Wall Street Jungle* (by John Rolfe and Peter Troob, published by Warner Books)

Two young MBA grads from Wharton and Harvard landed investment banking jobs at what was then a Wall Street powerhouse—Donaldson, Lufkin & Jenrette—straight out of school. Originally lured into the business by dreams of wealth, power, and prestige, their tale is a sobering story of the life of I-banking associates (grunt labour, huge hours, no social lives, and egomaniac bosses).

16. *Valuation: Measuring and Managing the Value of Companies* (by McKinsey & Company Inc., et al., published by John Wiley & Sons)

McKinsey & Company's guide to corporate valuation brings together concepts from corporate strategy and finance.

CHAPTER

# Equity Capital Markets
# PROFESSIONAL

# CHAPTER 6

# Equity Capital Markets Professional

## Overview

THE EQUITY CAPITAL MARKETS (ECM) group, which is called *syndication* at some independent firms, essentially plays the role of a quarterback when an investment dealer brings an equity issue to market. An ECM professional acts as a hub between investment banking, institutional sales/trading, the lawyers, and the other syndicate members.

One equity capital markets professional simplifies and describes the ECM function best by using an analogy to a T-shirt vendor: The T-shirt vendor has to buy inventory/product, price the product correctly so it sells well, and make any necessary markdowns to unsold inventory in order to get it sold, leaving the vendor with as little risk of losing money as possible. The ECM job is virtually the same except that ECM professionals sell stocks rather than T-shirts.

In reality, however, it does get more involved. I-bankers manage the corporate client relationships, prepare the offering documents, and crunch the numbers, while the ECM professionals are the product experts for equity and equity-related financings (whereas debt capital markets professionals are the product experts for fixed-income deals). They are responsible for assessing trends in the equity markets, working in an origination capacity and pitching equity deals, identifying client demand/interest for equity products, creating sales/marketing documents, planning and managing road shows for equity offerings, pricing equity deals, and providing after-market feedback.

Although the ECM role is definitely one of the best jobs on Bay Street, keep in mind that:

• The ECM job is a second-generation and sometimes third-generation job, meaning that one has to get into the business first and excel at that first or second job (typically I-banking) before even being considered for an ECM role.

• There are only 60 or so of these positions in the country, whereas there are at least ten times that number of investment banking jobs.

### Education

The educational requirements for this role tend to vary depending on the type of firm.

Since the domestic bank-owned dealers tend to recruit their ECM junior professionals from the investment banking associate ranks, we simply look at the educational backgrounds of young I-bankers. As noted in the previous chapter, investment banking associates typically have undergraduate business/economics or law degrees as well as MBAs.

Several of the independent firms, on the other hand, have hired their ECM/syndication professionals from the operations side of the firm. On that side of the business, the educational backgrounds of the individuals range from college degrees to university undergraduate degrees.

## Compensation

ECM professionals'compensation trends tend to be highly correlated to the volume of equity deals done by their firm. The number of deals led, personal performance, tenure, and market/street value also weigh in as inputs into the compensation decisions, but are secondary to the deal volume.

Junior ECM professionals (i.e., at the associate level) at bank-owned dealers tend to be compensated at the higher end of the range of what they would earn as an associate in investment banking. Typically, an I-banking associate would get paid an annual base salary of approximately $75,000 to $85,000, and the annual bonus could be anywhere from double to triple the base salary. An ECM associate bonus would more than likely be at the higher end of that range.

At the most senior levels, however, that dynamic is reversed. The most senior I-bankers (the rainmakers) tend to get paid more than the most senior ECM professionals. The logic is simple: in Bay Street's pay-for-performance culture, the ones *bringing in* the deals will always be paid more than the ones *executing* them.

All the levels in between associate and managing director (i.e., associate directors, directors, and executive directors) are compensated in about the same range as their counterparts in investment banking.

## Industry Certification

Having the CFA designation is highly recommended. The CFA designation has become the standard in the investment/finance industry. The program may or may not make you a better ECM/syndication professional, but successful completion of the program has become a rite of passage into the institutional equity community.

To earn the CFA charter, a CFA candidate must pass three six-hour examinations (CFA Institute suggests that 250 hours of study is needed to prepare for each exam) and have spent three years working in a role where he or she is involved in the investment decision-making process.

The average pass rate for each of the exams tends to hover around 50%. Of the approximately 56,000 CFA charterholders worldwide, few have passed all three exams consecutively.

## The Job

To understand the equity capital markets/syndication role, we first look at the primary functions performed by the group and then put some of the daily activities into the context of a bought deal financing.

**Origination.** The process of pitching to get the business, or *sourcing the deal*, is probably the most creative part of the deal process. The real art here is being able to "call the market"— the ability to bring a good idea to the right client at the right time. In timing a deal (for general growth purposes versus acquisition financing), the trick is not providing money when the company *needs* it, but when the market is willing to *provide* it.

This market shrewdness takes years to develop and as such, the ECM professionals responsible for the origination function are the most senior team members. Typically, when the investment bankers (usually one to three individuals) go to pitch a corporate client on an equity financing, they bring a senior ECM professional to the meeting.

**Structuring.** Structuring refers to creating a financing product/solution that suits the needs of investors in the context of market conditions. A solution can be product-driven (equity versus debt or a combination of both) or choosing the private markets versus the public markets (private placement versus IPO).

**Syndication**. In a broader context, *syndication* can mean ensuring the smooth transition of a financing, from deal pricing to deal closing. As an individual function, it means offering participation in a deal/financing to other dealers. In a bought deal, where a firm commits its own capital to underwrite the transaction, the act of offering participation to other dealers and putting a syndicate together is simply for insurance—to share the risk. However, with a marketed deal—an agency transaction—there is less incentive to syndicate. In fact, a firm would syndicate as little as possible.

In putting a syndicate together, the lead manager on the deal tries to pick strong partners (i.e., firms that may have a particular strength that the lead manager may not have in terms of being able to sell their portion of the deal). Typically, a syndicate wants at least one member to have a meaningful retail network/component and perhaps another member to have strong institutional client relationships outside of Canada, and some ECM professionals have been known to try to get the firm whose analyst has an opposing view into the deal.

**Execution and marketing**. This is the process from drafting the preliminary prospectus to closing the deal. This includes activities such as rehearsing the road shows with the management team, managing the institutional and retail road show schedule, and circulating documents/data to several audiences: syndicate members, internal sales forces (both institutional and retail), investment banking, and the corporate client.

**Pricing**. One of the most challenging functions in the whole process, this is where the most senior of the ECM professionals get involved. The pricing exercise is a fine balancing act. On the one hand, you have the corporate issuer's expectations (issuers want to set as high a price as possible so that they raise more money). On the other hand, you have the institutional (and retail) clients' expectations (clients want the deal priced as low as possible so they have more upside).

The institutional clients tend to be price-sensitive and are therefore the price-setters in the process. Retail clients, who can account for between 20% and 50% of a deal, are typically insensitive to price and are therefore price-takers— they put in orders for volume with no price constraints. The retail clients, however, are looked after by virtue of the institutions doing their homework and driving the best price for all buyers.

In pricing an equity deal, a wide number of factors are taken into consideration. It takes years of capital markets experience and a well-developed market sense to properly evaluate and weigh the following inputs in setting the final price on a deal:

- valuations of precedent deals and how easily/well they sold
- recent block trades and the prices at which the trades were done
- sectoral accumulation (which sector is hot?)
- yield
- recent analyst reports and changes in estimates/ recommendations
- recent quarterly earnings numbers
- use of proceeds
- market/investor sentiment (what the market appetite is for different sectors)
- equity fund flows

- institutional demand

- retail demand

**Allocation.** Quite simply put, allocation means cutting up the pie, or distributing stock to fill clients' orders.

**After-market support.** After the deal is done, the ECM group collects and provides market intelligence to the corporate client.

> "The most important aspect of the job one learns only by being on the job—a good market sense."
> —*Marilia Costa, Equity Capital Markets, Orion Securities Inc.*

### The Bought Deal

In Canada, all initial public offerings are fully-marketed deals. However, for follow-on common share financings, the majority of deals (up to 80%, as suggested by industry participants) are bought deals.

*Evolution of a Common Stock Bought Deal*

**9:00 a.m.**   Investment bankers have final talk with company management about the potential bought deal and proposed terms (e.g., size of the deal, pricing of the deal, syndicate splits, etc.). The discussion between the bankers and company management has been going on for weeks.

**1:00 p.m.**   The ECM group prepares a syndicate package with term sheet, timelines, etc.

**2:30 p.m.**   Investment bankers submit a firm bought deal letter and term sheet to the corporate client.

**2:45 p.m.**   Company management convenes a board meeting.

| | |
|---|---|
| **3:00 p.m.** | If the terms—principally size and price—are acceptable, the company signs the engagement letter and sends it back to the investment dealer. |
| **3:05 p.m.** | The ECM group emails syndicate members to notify them of a syndicate meeting. |
| **3:15 p.m.** | Syndicate meeting begins. This is a conference call between syndicate members to go through the term sheet (number of shares, size of deal, deal price, closing date and proposed splits, etc.) between the members. |
| **3:20 p.m.** | The ECM group sends the press release to news services so they can prepare it for the launch of the deal. |
| **3:21 p.m.** | Company counsel calls market surveillance at the TSX to notify them that the lead underwriter has a signed engagement letter and to halt the stock. |
| **3:30 p.m.** | Stock is halted. |
| **3:31 p.m.** | The ECM group calls the news services to give approval to release the details of the bought deal to the newswire system. |
| **3:35 p.m.** | The ECM group communicates to both the syndicate and the internal sales forces (retail and institutional) that the deal is live. |
| **3:40 p.m.** | The ECM allocates the retail portion of the deal (typically 20% to 50%) to other syndicate members. |
| **3:45 p.m.** | For the next hour or so, the institutional sales desk calls the institutional accounts to pitch the deal and the book of orders starts to build. |
| **5:00 p.m.** | The institutional desk has finished making its calls and the order book closes. |
| **5:15 p.m.** | The ECM group sits down with the head of equities to allocate stock to the institutional accounts. The allocation (or "fill") that any account gets depends on how quickly they showed interest in participating on the deal |

and the "quality" of that client (how consistently do they play in the sector?). The issuer wants good, knowledge-able institutional shareholders in a deal.

## A Day in the Life of a Head of ECM at an Independent Firm

**Marilia Costa**, managing director at Orion Securities Inc., is head of Equity Capital Markets at the firm. Ms. Costa has been in the business since 1990 and has been running the ECM depart-ment at Orion since 1996.

It's kind of interesting how I ended up in the equity capital markets role. After graduating from college, I landed a job at First Marathon Securities in the oper-ations (back-office support) side of the firm. I ended up working in three different departments over the course of two years. Then one day I noticed a couple of new internal job postings. One of the postings was for a syndication assistant working with and for the head of syndication. The way the job description was written did not make the job sound appealing to me, so I applied for the other one. A few days later, the head of syndication noticed me working on a project and called me. We met and she outlined what the job was really about and we had a good discussion about the responsibilities and her expectations. She called me later that afternoon and offered me the job. (Getting ahead on Bay Street can be pretty random sometimes, so you just work hard and hope that you're in the right place at the right time.)

A couple of years into the job, my boss left the firm to take a sabbatical. I was left to sink or swim. The following year was an exceptional learning expe-rience, as I got more involved with dealing with the investment bankers, the institutional sales/trading desk, corporate clients, and lawyers. I was involved with allocations, syndicate calls, everything. To give credit where it is due, though, I was well-prepared for the challenge because the head of syndication that hired and trained me was an outstanding and dynamic teacher and mentor.

Half a year after my former boss left First Marathon, she joined a new firm. I was hoping to go over to the new firm to work with her again. But as we worked together on a financing where both our firms were part of the syndicate, it became apparent to both of us that I could do the role on my own and no longer needed a senior person above me.

Shortly thereafter, a couple of senior investment bankers from Midland Walwyn were now at Yorkton Securities, the predecessor firm to Orion Securities, and needed syndication expertise. They called my former First Marathon boss and she recommended me for the job. The opportunity offered more room for growth and I was up for a new challenge, so I took the job. They encouraged me to hire a second person immediately. Finding a good number-two person is not easy. The person has to be balanced in that they have to be extremely competent and capable of supporting the lead person but content with being the backup with much less (if any) client exposure.

My role as head of equity capital markets at Orion has evolved over the years. It was a great experience and an exciting time to be here in a tech/biotech boutique as we went through a wild tech market and then as the firm evolved into one that focuses on five sectors. There's lots of adrenaline and that, to me, is the best part of the job. Good ideas seem to flow best when the adrenaline is flowing!

My typical day as head of ECM at an independent firm might look like this:

**7:30 a.m.**   Begin my day with going through the business newspapers in my office while listening to the morning meeting.

**8:00 a.m.**   Go into the morning meeting to talk about deals that we are marketing and gather feedback from our sales force regarding the meetings between the issuers and the institutional accounts.

**8:30 a.m.**   Head back to my office and prepare for our weekly corporate finance meeting. I review and gather information on all deals that are currently being marketed, and bought deals that have been done over the last week, both at Orion and by all other dealers.

**9:00 a.m.**   Attend our corporate finance meeting and report revenue visibility for the month, as well as give the group a summary of all new issues. I talk about deals that have been completed since our last meeting and deals that are still in marketing. I report which deals have done well and which ones haven't gone so well. I also talk about missed opportunities with the group. We talk about potential new business for the duration of the meeting.

**10:00 a.m.**   Go back to my office and return calls that I've missed while in the CF meeting. I get a call from banker #1 to discuss a potential bought deal. I ask the banker to meet in my office. I then call our head of sales so we can all discuss the opportunity. In the meeting we go over market conditions for the specific sector, whether or not we believe there will be enough demand for this stock, look at recent blocks, upcoming news that may impact this company, talk about use of proceeds, and look at how well other deals in this sector have been received. We all agree that the market tone for this particular sector is not strong enough and we will continue to monitor the market and the stock until the tone improves. At this point I have no need to call a bought deal meeting with a larger group.

**10:30 a.m.**   I call each salesperson individually to get direct feedback from institutional meetings and gather orders to start building the book for a fully marketed IPO we are working on. I call the banker and summarize the deal status so that he can inform the issuer that the book is building nicely.

**11:00 a.m.**   Call other syndicate members that are in our IPO to get their updated retail interest, and to give them a summary of how the deal is going.

**11:15 a.m.**   Receive call from banker #2 to talk about a bought deal opportunity in his sector. The same group as mentioned earlier meet in my office again to go over the same criteria. We all agree that with this company we should put up a bought deal letter. I call a bought deal/liability meeting for 11:45 a.m. with a larger group of people consisting of our head trader, head liability trader, head of sales, head of corporate finance, our CFO/COO, head of research, corporate finance relationship manager, and our analyst that covers the stock.

**11:45 a.m.**   I chair the bought deal committee meeting and go over the committee memo. I review the potential terms, the trading stats including block trades over the last year, month, and week, research coverage on the street, previous financings that this company has completed, capital requirements for our firm, potential syndicate composition, and timing of this deal. We then discuss price and our confidence in the deal clearing the market. This part of the meeting is turned over to sales and trading for their input on market intelligence. We all agree to put up a firm bought deal letter to the company. Banker #2 is now off to call the company and start discussions with them.

**12:15 p.m.** Review bought deal letter that is to be presented to the company and give my input to our CF department.

**12:30 p.m.** Off to a client lunch with another banker to meet with a potential new IPO client. We discuss Orion's market intelligence and our ability to lead their IPO. Client also wants to discuss syndicate composition and get our thoughts on other dealers that will bring value to the table.

**1:30 p.m.** Get a call from banker #2 indicating that his client is very interested in our bought deal letter and that they are going to call a board meeting.

**2:00 p.m.** Get back to the office and am told that we are going to lead the deal and the company would like to go live this afternoon. While our banker, lawyers, and the client negotiate the details of the engagement, I start preparing for the launch of our deal. I review the syndicate book, press release, and all other relevant documentation.

**2:15 p.m.** A syndicate meeting is called for 2:45 p.m. I call the TSX and discuss the deal that may hit the market in the afternoon and advise that minor details are still being negotiated.

**2:30 p.m.** I go back to the investment banking department and check on status. No major issues are outstanding. I speak with the lawyers and the client to go over some last-minute details.

**2:45 p.m.** Back in my office, I get on the syndicate conference call to go over the bought deal terms with the dealers that we are inviting into the deal. Syndicate members are advised of their syndicate percentage and I discuss Orion's views on why we believe the deal will clear the market. I ask that everyone get back to me by no later than 3:15 p.m. so that we can get signed up and hit the market by 3:30 p.m.

**3:00 p.m.** I start getting calls back from each syndicate member accepting their position in the deal. At this point I give dealers their retail allocation and let them know that I will contact them when we are live. I advise our banker that all of the dealers have accepted and I ask him to get the letter signed up.

**3:20 p.m.**    Deal is signed by both parties, so I call the TSX and let them know. They halt the stock.

**3:25 p.m.**    Press release goes out. We are now able to get on the phone and get orders. Our desk and our syndicate are advised that we are live.

**3:30 p.m.**    I collect orders from Orion's institutional desk to build the book. Calls are coming in from other dealers that aren't in our deal who want to get shares, but they are informed that we will not be forming a selling group since our book is already building and I don't anticipate having room for them. Our syndicate members are all calling for more retail stock and some are calling in institutional orders for our book.

**4:00 p.m.**    Book is now oversubscribed, so I go out to the desk and try and determine the number of accounts that we are still waiting to hear from. I determine that we should be in a position to close the books by 4:45 (I know it will be 5:00 by the time we actually hear back from everyone). I call the syndicate to tell them that we are closing books at 4:45 and get an update on how much retail demand they have.

**5:00 p.m.**    I am now certain that we have heard back from all of the accounts and I sit down with our head of sales to carve up the book (do the allocations). This is proving to be a very difficult task. From our initial cut, it doesn't look like we are going to be able to make any one account happy. We decide to call up our banker and have him go back to the company and ask them to increase the size of the deal, because the deal is extremely oversubscribed and we all feel that the company will make good use of the proceeds. After making this call, we run a second set of allocations based on the increased deal size. Since the accounts are all waiting for their fills, we have to get allocations out as soon as we hear back from our banker.

**5:15 p.m.**  Client has agreed to increase the deal size. I fire off the allocations to our desk, and they call the accounts with their allotments. I call each syndicate member and advise them of the deal increase and put out more retail shares. A second press release goes out announcing that the deal is being increased.

**5:45 p.m.**  Call the banker and give him feedback on the deal so that he can advise the client. From our desk, I get feedback from the clients that they want more shares if possible.

**6:00 p.m.**  Return the numerous calls that I was unable to take when I was busy with our deal, and tie up some loose ends on a deal that we have closing in the morning.

**7:00 p.m.**  Head over to a closing dinner to celebrate a previously closed transaction.

**8:30 p.m.**  Receive a call from another syndicate member informing me that there is going to be a syndicate meeting at 7:30 a.m. the next morning. I have no idea what the deal is; all I know is that Orion's liability is going to be meaningful. I excuse myself from the table, quickly get my committee on stand-by for the next morning, and advise them of our liability.

**9:00 p.m.**  Go back to the table and enjoy the rest of the evening.

**10:30 p.m.**  Finally, I'm on my way home to see my family and get some sleep.

# HOW ECM ASSOCIATES SPEND THEIR TIME

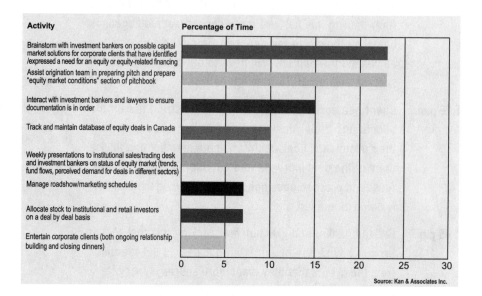

| Activity | Percentage of Time |
| --- | --- |

Source: Kan & Associates Inc.

The above percentages tend to change depending on:

- **Deal flow.** When the ECM group has several deals that are live, the focus is on executing those transactions, so naturally more time is spent on managing the road show/marketing schedules, doing the documentation, and allocating the stock. The brainstorming/pitching efforts are reduced until the live transactions have closed.

- **Whether the associate's firm is the bookrunner.** The responsibility of executing/processing a transaction rests with the bookrunner, so therefore the bookrunner's associates are the ones liaising with lawyers, accountants, and company management on preparation of offering documents, participating in due diligence sessions, etc., whereas the syndicate members' associates may simply get on the syndicate call.

## A Chat with a Head of ECM
## at a Bank-Owned Dealer

**Wayne Adlam**, managing director at CIBC World Markets, is head of the firm's Equity Capital Markets group. He was previously co-head of CIBC World Markets Capital, the firm's merchant banking arm.

**Q. How did you get your start in the business?**

A. My first job after completing my MBA was in the finance group at Ford Motor Company. After approximately a year at Ford, a former MBA classmate of mine gave me a call. He was with Wood Gundy's investment banking group in Calgary and they needed another associate. I met with the senior bankers in their office, and after a few chats/interviews they offered me the job.

**Q. What did you like most about the investment banking experience?**

A. I liked dealing with the corporate clients. But it wasn't just dealing with clients for the sake of dealing with clients. As part of a tier one dealer that led a lot of transactions, I met and interacted with some of the most high-profile names in corporate Canada at the time. Furthermore, our firm's spot near the top of the Bay Street pecking order allowed us to work on many headline transactions. It was a good feeling to open up the business newspapers and see the spotlight on a big transaction that our team worked on, and we would know much more about the dynamics and nuances of the deal than the article had space to delve into.

**Q. What lessons did you take away from your investment banking experience?**

A. I took away two lessons:

1. Learn to work smart. Time is of the essence in this business, so you have to learn to make good decisions on imperfect information. It's not enough to work hard or work long hours—the best professionals know how to work smart.

2. Always focus on the client. Think about the client. Talk about the client. It's more than just good business practice; it's what differentiates top producers in our business. The best professionals are viewed by the client as always looking out for their best interests.

**Q.    Which of your other experiences in life best prepared you for your equity capital markets role?**

A.    The Western MBA (with its case method) prepared me well for being an investment banker. I found that the banking job was just like doing cases. And then it was a fundamental grounding in investment banking that prepared me well for ECM. The things that one learns in investment banking are critical to being a good equity capital markets professional: being able to read and interpret financial statements quickly, having a thorough understanding of the capital markets process, and under-standing securities laws (e.g., prospectus requirements).

**Q.    What do you look for when hiring an equity capital markets associate?**

A.    We look for young investment bankers with two to three years of experience. I'm not as concerned about the title (i.e., whether it's a second- or third-year analyst or a first-year associate) as I am about getting the cream of the crop. ECM associates will need to take a leadership role in their position so we tend to look for young I-bankers that stand out and have the respect of their peers. Furthermore, we look for bankers that have spent a disproportionate amount of their time working on equity financings (as opposed to M&A assignments). As well, we look for candidates with a good market sense—someone who's a student of the market.

**Q. What advice would you give to someone aspiring to get a job with an ECM group?**

A. If the person is just coming out of MBA school and wants to break into our business, my first thought is to give a few words of encouragement: Getting the first job on the Street is tough but once you're in, you're in. Once you've been given the stamp of approval by one firm, you'll be employable at other firms. In terms of advice to someone looking to get into ECM, I would just highlight how few ECM jobs there are in Canada (probably around 60 professionals), so one should be realistic about landing a spot with an ECM group. Think about it this way—how many pre-business students at Western actually get into the business program?

**Profile of the Ideal Equity Capital Markets Professional**

The ideal ECM professional should have the following attributes:

- strong interpersonal skills
- strong personal presence
- good leadership qualities
- an excellent customer service ethic
- good product knowledge
- a good market sense
- a strong sense of urgency
- solid organizational skills
- detail-oriented
- tenacity
- an interest and understanding of financial markets

## The Largest Equity Capital Markets Teams in Canada*

| Firm | Number of Team Members |
|------|------------------------|
| 1. BMO NesbittBurns | 9 |
| 2. CIBC World Markets | 9 |
| 3. TD Newcrest | 9 |
| 4. RBC Capital Markets | 8 |
| 5. Scotia Capital Markets | 6 |
| 6. Merrill Lynch Canada | 5 |
| 7. National Bank Financial | 4 |

* measured by number of ECM/syndication professionals
(All other firms have one ECM/syndication professional.)

## 2003's Top Equity Dealmakers in Canada

| Underwriter | Total Number | Total Amount (in Millions of Dollars) |
|-------------|--------------|---------------------------------------|
| 1. CIBC World Markets | 15 | 12,910 |
| 2. RBC Capital Markets | 58 | 6,292 |
| 3. Scotia Capital | 56 | 5,407 |
| 4. BMO Nesbitt Burns | 52 | 3,599 |
| 5. TD Securities | 30 | 2,160 |
| 6. Merrill Lynch Canada | 8 | 1,521 |
| 7. National Bank Financial | 27 | 1,460 |
| 8. UBS Securities Canada | 5 | 1,272 |
| 9. GMP Securities | 66 | 1,254 |
| 10. Canaccord Capital | 103 | 1,053 |
| 11. Salomom Smith Barney | 5 | 842 |
| 12. Orion Securities | 36 | 510 |
| 13. Morgan Stanley & Co. | 3 | 421 |
| 14. Dundee Securities | 34 | 323 |
| 15. Haywood Securities | 43 | 304 |
| 16. FirstEnergy Capital | 28 | 303 |
| 17. Banc of America Securities | 2 | 296 |

| | | |
|---|---|---|
| 18. Peters & Co. | 16 | 285 |
| 19. Sprott Securities | 12 | 273 |
| 20. Raymond James | 19 | 247 |

Source: *National Post*

## Suggested Reading

1. *Applied Corporate Finance: A User's Manual* (by Aswath Damodaran, published by John Wiley & Sons)

   Written by an NYU Stern Business School finance professor, this text focuses on converting financial theory into practical financial analysis.

2. *Barbarians at the Gate* (by Bryan Burrough and John Helyar, published by Harper Business)

   A business book classic, this narrative of the leveraged buyout of RJR Nabsico Corp. for $25 billion underscores the greed and excesses of the '80s.

3. *Bigwig Briefs: Become an Investment Banker: The Real World Intelligence Necessary to Become a Successful Investment Banker* (by Aspatore Books Staff, published by Aspatore Books)

   Interviews with 10 "bigwigs" (six investment bankers and four venture capitalists). The book doesn't give any advice on becoming an investment banker but does give some insight into what investment bankers do.

4. *The Business of Investment Banking* (by K. Thomas Liaw, published by John Wiley & Sons)

This is a good overview of the investment banking business and the key trends affecting the future of the business.

5. *Corporate Finance: A Valuation Approach* (by Simon Z. Benninga and Oded Sarig, published by McGraw–Hill/ Irwin)

This text provides a good introduction into the valuation of assets, companies, and individual securities. It provides step-by-step guidance toward company valuation and building financial models.

6. *Damodaran on Valuation: Security Analysis for Investment and Corporate Finance* (by Aswath Damodaran, published by John Wiley & Sons)

The NYU Stern Business School finance professor provides a good overview of three valuation approaches for investment analysis: discounted cash flow, relative valuation, and contingent claim valuation.

7. *Doing Deals: Investment Banks at Work* (by Robert G. Eccles and Dwight B. Crane, published by Harvard Business School Press)

Executives from several major Wall Street investment banks reveal their firms' management practices. Although slightly dated, one can still glean some insights into the structure of the industry, how bonuses are determined, relationship management issues, etc.

8. *Financial Modeling*—2nd Edition (by Simon Benninga and Benjamin Czaczkes, published by MIT Press)

This is a good book on the fundamentals of spreadsheet modelling using Excel.

9. *Handbook of Canadian Security Analysis, Volumes I & II* (edited by Joe Kan, published by John Wiley & Sons)

   This valuable reference is a guide to evaluating the industry sectors of the market. Some 28 of Canada's top-ranked sell-side analysts were hand-picked to share their expertise and experience in understanding and analyzing the fundamental forces that drive stock performance in each industry group.

10. *Investment Valuation: Tools and Techniques for Determining the Value of Any Asset* (by Aswath Damodaran, published by John Wiley & Sons)

    Another book by the NYU finance professor, this is a comprehensive guide for determining the value of both financial assets (stocks, bonds, options, futures) and real assets (real estate).

11. *Masters of the Universe: Winning Strategies of America's Greatest Deal Makers* (by Daniel J. Kadlec, published by Harper Business)

    *Time* magazine's Wall Street columnist profiles nine of the biggest dealmakers of our era and profiles the most important, headline-grabbing deal of each's career.

12. *Monkey Business: Swinging Through the Wall Street Jungle* (by John Rolfe and Peter Troob, published by Warner Books)

    Two young MBA grads from Wharton and Harvard landed investment banking jobs at what was then a Wall Street powerhouse—Donaldson, Lufkin & Jenrette—straight out of school. Originally lured into the business by dreams of wealth, power, and prestige, their tale is a sobering story of the life of I-banking associates (grunt labour, huge hours, no social lives, and egomaniac bosses).

13. *Valuation: Measuring and Managing the Value of Companies* (by McKinsey & Company Inc., et al., published by John Wiley & Sons)

McKinsey & Company's guide to corporate valuation brings together concepts from corporate strategy and finance.

# 7
CHAPTER

# Venture
# **CAPITALIST**

# CHAPTER 7

# Venture Capitalist

## Overview

THE VENTURE CAPITAL (VC) FUNDING PROCESS is perhaps capitalism at its finest. An entrepreneur with a cutting-edge idea or invention shows a business plan to a venture capitalist. The venture capitalist injects some financing and helps grow the company by providing strategic and financial advice (in exchange for a piece of the action). Then the venture capitalist guides the company towards a liquidity event (either sells the company or takes the company public) for a five or ten-bagger five years later. It is a win-win-win-win situation—the company founder's entrepreneurial dream is transformed into a reality, the investors make above-average returns, the venture capitalists make impressive returns, and the I-bankers get their fees.

The role of a venture capitalist is varied. A venture capitalist will source the deal/investment, negotiate the deal, do due diligence/research, syndicate the deal, close the transaction, sit on the board of directors, and ultimately exit the deal.

In the private equity space (the financing of non-public companies), venture capitalists tend to focus on companies involved in the "new economy" (e.g., life sciences and technology). Venture capitalists often evaluate any given business case for advancing a product, so technology drives the investment decision. They place emphasis on company creation and are therefore involved in seed or early-stage rounds of financing. A typical investment is in the range of $2-$10 million, but can vary widely depending on the size of the fund.

Contrast a venture capitalist with a merchant banker who tends to focus on companies involved in the "old economy" (e.g., manufacturing). Old economy companies are likely more mature and established; therefore, the financials drive the investment decision. Merchant bankers are typically involved in later rounds of financing (e.g., mezzanine financing), with a typical investment in the range of $20-$100 million.

The VC community in Canada is small, with most firms located in Toronto, Montreal, Vancouver, and the Ottawa Valley. The largest firms have approximately 20 investment professionals, but most VC firms have 5 to 10 professional staffers. According to the Canadian Venture Capital Association (CVCA), there are approximately 850 venture capital and private equity professionals in the country.

Despite its relatively small size, the VC industry has been quite active. According to MacDonald and Associates, in 2003, Canadian VC firms had C$22.4 billion under management and invested C$1.5 billion into 616 businesses, down from C$22.5 billion under management with $2.5 billion distributed to 681 companies in 2002.

Compare the Canadian numbers to those of the U.S. VC industry. Thomson Venture Economics says that in 2003, U.S. VC firms disbursed US$18.2 billion to 2,235 businesses, down from $21.4 billion to 2,552 companies in 2002.

## Education

The education required of candidates for venture capital roles will differ depending on which fund he or she will be working on and on the firm's focus. According to MacDonald and Associates, the bulk of the funding in Canada is for knowledge-based industries like information technology (IT) and life sciences. In 2003, 47% of VC funds was distributed to IT companies, while 30% went to life sciences outfits. If you're thinking about going into the VC business, it would definitely be to your advantage to be tech or biotech savvy.

Professionals that end up working on the IT side of venture capital tend to be tech savvy, with strong financial acumen (e.g., an electrical engineer with an MBA). IT funds typically bring in outside technical consultants to evaluate new technologies/innovations.

For the life sciences team, undergraduate studies in health sciences (e.g., biology or chemistry) is a requirement. It would be difficult for someone without that background to even get through the executive summary of a new business plan proposal. However, financial modelling is not as important a skill in venture capital, since most companies at this early stage are cash-flow negative and likely do not even have sales revenues.

In the traditional low-tech end of the spectrum where companies are likely to have cash flow, financial modelling skills are more important, so a finance background is preferred.

"In the old days, a good venture capitalist was likely a good business person (with a good network of business contacts, a strong sense of business strategy and maybe some financial acumen) who had run a successful business themself. Today, a good VC *has* to have a strong technical underpinning because the science matters much more."

—*David MacNaughtan, Senior Vice President, Business Development, Drug Royalty Corporation*

### Compensation Range

Compensation in the VC world depends on where you are in the economic/market cycle. In the good years (when equity markets are strong), a venture capital firm will likely monetize some of its investments by exiting several of its investee companies through an IPO or sale, and in the process earn the senior venture capitalists some very lucrative paydays. However, it is a cyclical business so it can be four to five years between market peaks, so compensation can fluctuate widely.

For the investment analyst role, compensation is a mix of base salary, typically $70,000–$100,000, plus a bonus up to $50,000.

At the director or investment manager level, compensation is a mix of base salary, typically $120,000–$175,000, plus a payout of the fund's profits, which could double the base salary.

For the most senior venture capitalists (partners and managing directors), compensation is a mix of base salary, typically $200,000–$325,000, plus a participating interest in the fund's (or funds') performance that could take the total compensation package to several million dollars.

To get a sense of how much a partner can make, it is worth understanding the economics of a VC firm. VC funds charge a management fee of 2% of the capital under administration. The fund also takes a cut (an incentive fee of 15%–20%) of the fund's profits above a given hurdle rate (e.g., 10%, or some formula of bond yield plus 4%–5%). Individual partners and managing directors can also be more motivated by having a defined proportion of the incentive fee. And furthermore, at private partnerships, the senior partners may have a personal stake in the fund(s) they manage.

### Industry Certification

Having the CFA designation is highly recommended. In the past, the CFA candidate program was dominated by public market-types (buy-side and sell-side analysts). More recently, however, the new generation of private equity professionals are finding more CFA charterholders amongst their ranks. The program may or may not make you a better venture capitalist, but successful completion of the program has become a rite of passage into the investment community.

## How Venture Capital Works

Why do entrepreneurs and/or start-up companies turn to this high-cost source of funding?

Entrepreneurs usually go first to family and friends for funds. When that well runs dry, they approach the local bank manager only to be told (or reminded) that banks lend against hard assets and with many of today's innovations/companies being knowledge-based (and therefore lacking hard assets), bank financing is not an option.

With traditional low-cost sources of capital unavailable, venture capital becomes the only source.

VC firms/funds can focus on:

- **Stage of product**. Scientific-proof-of-principle stage versus commercial-proof-of-principle stage.

- **Company development**. Start-ups versus more mature companies (there is some overlap between this criterion and the previous one since the stage of the company typically reflects the stage of the product).

- **Stage of investment**. Seed investment (start-up of new venture) versus early stage (developing new products/services but have not yet proven those products/services in their markets) versus later-stage mezzanine (companies that are commercially viable and pre-IPO).

- **Geography/region—province or region**. Venture capitalists tend to invest in ventures in the same geographic area because of the time they actually spend with those ventures.

- **Industry/sector**. Life sciences versus information technology.

- **Low-tech (manufacturing) or high tech (technology intensive)**.

Venture capitalists take a meaningful stake in their investee companies (up to 40%) and sometimes more in early-stage investments (up to 60%), but this stake is diluted down with each successive round of financing. The VC (and the syndicate) rarely take more than 60% of the equity in order to leave enough equity (and therefore incentive) for the company management team. This equity stake is usually taken in the form of preferred stock (and sometimes convertible debt). Theoretically, preferred stock represents a liquidation preference where the latest series of preferreds gets taken care of first in the event of bankruptcy. It is a last-in-first-out (LIFO) concept, where the investors in the last round of financing have the least information and therefore should be protected and be able to get their money out first. In reality, there is often a negotiated settlement between the venture capitalists involved.

This form of investment provides downside protection and upside participation (through the equity component). It is this potential upside that motivates venture capitalists to be not just a source of funds but also a value enhancer. Venture capitalists then act more like business developers, rolling up their sleeves and actively helping their investee companies succeed in the marketplace.

In taking a meaningful stake in portfolio companies, venture capitalists will at a minimum take an active monitoring role, while at the extreme will exercise influence on the company's operations and strategy by taking a seat on the board of directors. Ideally, a board would consist of the CEO, one (possibly two) venture capitalists from each series/round of financing, and two or three industry representatives. Typically, VC representation on the boards goes to the VC firm(s) with the largest capital commitment or to the lead investor on a given round. Interestingly, venture capitalists have the right to attend board meetings even if they are not on the board.

Networking is an integral part of the job. It is necessary to source deals, to be known to peers at competitors, and to have the best service providers (lawyers, accountants, consultants, investment bankers, etc.).

There is a misconception that venture capitalists work fast and loose throwing money at promising, but risky, ventures in the hopes of hitting a home run. In reality, VC firms tend to have disciplined screening mechanisms with which to choose investments. A venture capitalist may get hundreds of business plan submissions a year, and first must weed through the many proposals and uncover those with the highest potential.

To start with, a venture capitalist will likely read through the executive summaries and may decide whether to take a meeting with the entrepreneurs. The screening process usually begins with determining the "area of focus." For example, a venture capital firm with a focus on life sciences may focus further on opportunities within certain sub-segments of the industry like biomaterials or central nervous system (CNS) drugs. Other screens include:

- **The stage of development**. VC firms tend to be focused on either seed, early-stage, or later-stage investing. A firm with a mandate to invest in seed-stage opportunities may not outright dismiss any company in the early-stage, but the opportunity would have to be compelling in order for the firm to invest.

- **The company's management team**. Ideally, venture capitalists like to back strong, capable management teams with a proven track record.

- **The market attractiveness.** Venture capitalists look at the market potential and the competitive landscape.

- **The company's or product's competitive advantage.** Is the team/company the first out of the gates with the concept or product? Is there a clear value proposition? How is this company/product going to overcome the obstacles that others haven't?

- **The potential internal rate of return (IRR).** Some VC firms have a target IRR that they would like to achieve on the portfolio. Other firms feel that a target IRR is deal specific, and look at the risk profile of the company/opportunity to determine the IRR hurdle. For example, for a later-stage company that is in the process of building market share, a minimum IRR in the mid-20s would be adequate. However, for an early-stage company, where there may still be a question about market adoption of the company's product, a premium return would be required. In the context of the whole portfolio, these firms tend to have an overall blended IRR hurdle of between 20%–30%.

## Why Invest in a Venture Capital Fund

A few reasons to invest in VC funds include:

1. **Diversification.** As an alternative asset class, returns on VC funds are uncorrelated with equities and other traditional asset classes. Furthermore, the risk in a fund is minimized through diversification within the fund and downside protection on individual investments in the form of the investment itself (i.e., preferred stock or convertible debenture).

2. **The VC fund manager's interests are aligned with those of the investors.** VC funds are similar to hedge

funds in that they both have base management fees (of approximately 2% based on the assets under management), but the real juice is the performance fees (typically 15%–20% of profits above some minimum return/hurdle rate). Fund managers earn lucrative incentive fees if they deliver good returns for the investors in their fund(s).

3. **To participate in the growth of early-stage companies.** VC funds give investors exposure to early-stage (information technology and life sciences) investments that investors could not make on their own. Venture capitalists should have a higher probability of identifying investments that are undervalued than the typical investor has. The returns from VC investments are theoretically superior since venture capitalists are often active investors and can influence management and the investment outcome.

## Why Work for a Venture Capital Fund

There are four main reasons to consider working for a VC fund. First, the relatively wide scope of work makes the job interesting. Throughout the life cycle of an investment (from finding the deal/investment through to the final exit), a venture capitalist tends to wear several of the hats of the public sector. In the initial phase of looking for potential investment opportunities, a VC does the work of a portfolio manager in reviewing and evaluating the merits of numerous business plans (although a portfolio manager tends to review public documents such as annual reports). During the due diligence/research phase of the process, a venture capitalist assumes the role of an analyst in doing the research on the industry, the market, the company, and the product/service. In the syndication phase, where a venture capitalist looks for co-investors on a deal, he wears the hat of an equity capital markets/syndication professional. During the final phase of trying to exit the investment by finding a potential acquirer or evaluating the potential for an IPO, the venture capitalist acts as an investment banker.

Second, there is extensive access to critical company information to make investment decisions. Venture capitalists tend to get total access to company information and management time. This is in contrast to public market investing, where investors are limited to publicly available information and therefore place their bets on incomplete company information.

Third, venture capitalists have the ability to play in both the private equity and public market arena. Although the primary focus of VC is private equity, most funds can invest up to 15% of the funds in public market deals as long as the stock is issued out of treasury.

Fourth, there is limitless income potential thanks to the performance-based fee structure at private VC firms. The industry works off a formula whereby the fund charges a 2% management fee for assets under management and a 15%–20% incentive fee on portfolio gains above some base level of return to investors.

## A Day in the Life of a
## Top Venture Capital Associate

**Tatiana Badescu**, CFA, was an investment analyst at VenGrowth Capital Partners (she is currently in the business development group at U.S. Energy Savings Corp.).

Bachelor of Arts (math) from York University, 1998

I landed my first job in venture capital almost by accident. I had no interest in venture capital at the time and had no idea what it was. My major during my undergraduate studies was in math so I didn't have the same drive to get into the investment industry as the business students.

I applied to the human resources department at the Royal Bank of Canada (RBC). RB Ventures (RBC's venture capital arm) had an internship position working on their website. I was sent in to see them since I had some experience in that area. I worked for the summer on that project, and during that time I got involved with the due diligence aspect of venture capital by helping out with financial modelling and research. At the end of the summer, RB Ventures made me an offer for a full-time position with their group as an investment analyst. During my brief summer stint, I found the VC world exciting and interesting, so I accepted the job.

Any initial reservations about whether my academic background would be adequate for the job were quickly dispelled. I found that my finance and accounting courses, and my ability to work with Excel, were all very useful (given that the basic duties of an analyst are financial modelling and research). I also enrolled in the CSC [Canadian Securities Course] and CFA [Chartered Financial Analyst] programs to expand my investment knowledge. The rest of the job I learned as I went—how to judge businesses, how to read legal agreements, how to do proper due diligence, etc.

I learned fairly quickly that venture capital is an aggressive, highly competitive business: It is a lot of money chasing a few good deals. I also learned that the business operates largely on the basis of personal integrity and trust. While competitive, venture capitalists stick together, work and eat at the same places, stay close to each other. Decisions that one helps to make may lead to millions of dollars of loss or profit for the firm and we are responsible for the lives of people whose jobs partially depend on what we decide. It just feels better to be with other colleagues in a similar situation.

My days are spent wrapped up in the opportunity recognition process: reading business plans, talking to management, researching markets and the competitive landscape, and searching for solid companies that need growth capital. All along the way I spend time thinking of ideas and bouncing them off of some very sharp people. I spend a large part of the job working alone, trying to wrap my head around a business. While much of the effort requires discussion and dialog, I sometimes go the whole day having spoken to only one or two people.

The schedule is pretty much 10–11 hour days, five days a week, with the occasional marathon night or weekend when a deal is closing. Most of the time is spent trying to figure out why a deal should be done. The critical lessons I have learned in this business are:

1. **Don't guess—know for certain.** If you guess, you might end up being wrong and will lose credibility, and possibly money.

2. **There's no substitute for doing the work.** Regardless of how much you know about a subject, there's always something you don't know that is perhaps more relevant to the situation. If you can't figure out what it is that you don't know, let the team know. When making a highly illiquid investment in a small, risky business, information asymmetry becomes a massive problem. It is absolutely critical that you know your limits and let the team know what they are.

3. **If you really like a deal, learn how to hate it.** If it is truly a good investment, you should be able to hate the business and still want to do the deal. This is harder than it sounds because in early-stage investing, there are many questions that remain unanswered and there is rarely enough hard data to do a credible quantitative analysis.

My typical day as an associate within a venture capital firm might look like this:

**7:45 a.m.**    Arrive at the office.

**8:00 a.m.**    Respond to e-mails and voicemails from the day before. I communicate primarily with entrepreneurs, other venture capitalists, and personal acquaintances within my network.

**9:00 a.m.**    Head over to the boardroom for a meeting with a group of entrepreneurs who want to pitch us on their new venture (I read the business plan the previous day). One general partner (GP) sits in with us. The other GP, who planned to be there, cannot make it because he has a conference call with a portfolio company facing some challenges. The new venture has already won some points with us—they were introduced to us by an agent with whom we've done work before, and who does a relatively good job of trying to introduce only companies that fit our investment criteria. As well, the entrepreneur already has a successful business and is personally investing in this new one. The goal of this presentation for us is to find out what major problems the product will solve in the marketplace. We want to see that the product is perhaps 10 times faster or somehow better than the competition, or that it fills an unmet need in the existing market. The presentation goes well, except it is a bit rich with technical details and industry jargon. However, it does a good job at focusing on how they will capture the market.

**10:30 a.m.**    I just received the financial model from another company we are looking at as a potential investment. It contains five years of projections. They also sent in their historical balance sheets and income and cash flow statements. I am looking to ensure that the projections are in line with the historical trends. (If the growth of the company has been averaging 15% per year, but the projections are showing 35% per year, we have to find out what has changed to allow for that.) I analyze all statements line by line. For example, the income statement should have expenses broken down into subgroups, such as sales and marketing, cost of goods sold, research and development, general administration, interest expense, and income tax expense. We need to understand how/why product pricing may change gross profit margins, why other expenses may change as a percentage of revenue, and what capital expenditures will be needed. We will also analyze the sales pipeline and the assumptions behind the cost structure to ensure that everything adds up. The company told us that they plan to hire a sales person and a marketing person in Month Three, and launch an advertising campaign in Month Four. We look to see if there are additional expenses linked to the two potential hires in the plan, such as phones, travel, desks, etc., and that advertising expenses have gone up in Month Four. On the balance sheet, I am looking to see if there are different series of common shares or if there is preferred stock outstanding. Once this detailed analysis is done, I can start thinking about valuing the company.

**12:00 p.m.**    Have lunch with an executive recruiter. This person is very experienced in finding management talent in our area of expertise. We've kept in touch over the years, and try to see each other every quarter to exchange the latest news. It is a fun lunch, freely mixing personal and professional information.

**1:45 p.m.** Back at the office. I start to work on the company that we saw this morning. I do the initial market and competitive analysis. The company showed us how they plan to penetrate the market; our job is to see how sound their approach is. I put all their marketing assumptions to the test. I think of who I know that can give me independent feedback. Then I see what research reports, industry analysts, and studies say about the market. Among the questions I need answered are: Is the market as big as they say? Will they be able to charge the price they plan to charge and be profitable? Is distribution as easy as they project? I then make my own assessment about the competition. If I find that another company may actually beat them to the market, the chances of us funding them decreases substantially if success was linked to being first out of the gate.

**3:30 p.m.** Make due diligence calls for a potential investment I have been following for two months. Last week I called the company's customers and suppliers, and they seemed happy for the most part. My goal was to obtain an independent assessment of the market and any market adoption problems that might come up. Today, I am calling the personal references of the management team. I need to uncover any potential character or personality flaws any member of the team may have. During the entire due diligence process I do a lot of hard work to make sure that a company is what it says it is.

**4:30 p.m.** For the rest of the day I review legal documents for this potential investment. We expect to close the deal in the next few weeks. The lawyers sent us draft number four of the documents. Both the GP and I will be reviewing them again. Our firm is the lead investor and the syndicate is made up of three venture capital firms. At the last moment the entrepreneurs are not comfortable signing the Reps and Warranties, and they consider that they should receive an additional 5% in stock options. All other terms have been negotiated. I will read the documents again to ensure that no other changes were made. I then rerun the capitalization table to assess the impact of an additional 5% in options pre- and post-investment, and I set up a call directly with the entrepreneurs to explain what each of the Reps and Warranties mean and try to understand where the problems are. The additional stock options should not be a problem if they are given pre-financing. With the Reps and Warranties you know which ones will be sticking points—they are the same ones at every closing. After a long call with the entrepreneurs, we come to an agreement on all points, so the deal is now proceeding towards closing.

## HOW VENTURE CAPITAL ANALYSTS SPEND THEIR TIME

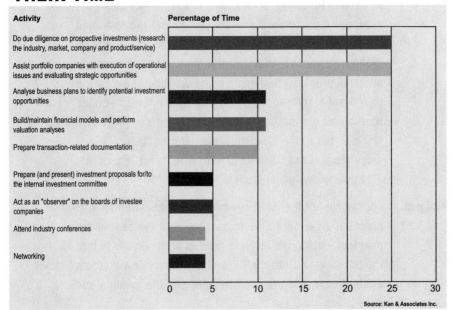

Source: Kan & Associates Inc.

**7:00 p.m.**   Run to catch the last train of the day. For reading material during the train ride home, I bring with me the latest research report covering a market that we are interested in.

The percentages in the opposite chart tend to change depending on:

- **Stage of the fund.** In the early years of a fund, the majority of an analyst's time (up to 80%) is spent analyzing business plans, doing due diligence on potential investments, building models, and preparing closing documentation, with little time spent with investee companies. As the fund's capital becomes fully invested and the investments mature, the time allocation is reversed, with the bulk of an analyst's time (over 50%) spent on assisting portfolio companies.

- **Stage of the company being invested in.** A venture capitalist that invests in early-stage companies spends much more time actively working with the companies. Therefore, a higher percentage of time is spent in ongoing contact with the founders/management teams.

- **Stage of the deal.** Although activities like negotiating deal terms/legal agreements and preparing proposals for the internal investment committee may be a small part of time spent during the course of a year, they can consume all of one's time when deals are closing.

- **Size of the VC firm.** Smaller shops may outsource part, or all, of the due diligence function.

## A Chat with a Senior Venture Capitalist

**Judy Blumstock** is a principal at Genesys Capital Partners, one of the largest Canadian-based venture capital firms exclusively focused on the health care and biotechnology industries. Prior to joining Genesys, Ms. Blumstock was a partner at RBC Capital Partners and director of bio/pharmaceutical research at Drug Royalty.

**Q. When you were in university, did you know what you wanted to do when you graduated?**

A. No. I had gone straight to business school down in New York after my undergrad in biology. When I graduated from Columbia University, I was not sure what I wanted to do, so a friend and I started a small business in New York City. We thought we needed VC funding so we met with a number of venture capitalists and raised $140,000, which was a lot of money to us at the time. Throughout the process, we had a chance to see venture capitalists in action and the VC world fascinated me. In the stock market, you invest in publicly traded companies, which tend to be relatively mature entities, whereas in venture capital, you invest in the germ of an idea, which was much more interesting to me.

Around that time, I met the two partners of a venture firm called JR Capital and they really inspired me. They didn't invest in my company, but gave me some good advice as well as a copy of a book they had written titled *Young Men with Unlimited Capital*, a fun, easy read (if you can get your hands on a copy because it's now out of print). The book tells the story of how the two young partners of JR Capital took out an ad in *The Wall Street Journal* titled "2 Young Men with Unlimited Capital" with the intention of funding good business plans. They ended up backing Woodstock!

**Q. So how did you get your start in the venture capital business?**

A. In the late '80s, I decided to return to Toronto. It was very difficult to find a job in the VC world so I took a couple of jobs with software firms before getting a big break. I landed a job at Drug Royalty (a company that buys royalty streams on drugs) as an analyst. My responsibilities included looking at drug markets, managing the due diligence process, doing competitive assessments, and doing the valuations—

responsibilities very similar to those of a VC analyst/associate. So after six good years at Drug Royalty, I decided to make the move to the VC side, and to leverage my skills best my goal was to do healthcare/biotech venture capital. Fortunately, a headhunter contact gave me a heads-up that RBC Capital Partners was looking for a professional to lead their healthcare efforts. I applied for and got the job.

**Q. What did you take away from the Drug Royalty experience?**

A. I can think of four things right off the top of my head:

- the importance/necessity of having lots of contacts

- the attention to detail required when reviewing legal documentation

- the importance of good advisors

- in the process of building models on companies, to question the underlying assumptions of others' models

**Q. Which of your business philosophies has contributed to your success?**

A. You know how in real estate they talk about location, location, location? Well, in early-stage venture capital, I believe that it's people, people, people. You have to find or build a strong management team and make an assessment of whether you can work with them over the long run.

**Q. Genesys Capital has done well in the three years that the firm's been up and running. What do you credit that to?**

A. Because our mandate is to invest at a very early stage, we have the ability to create proprietary deal flow. In other words, we may identify a market opportunity, and we then find and hire the right scientific and management team to exploit the opportunity.

**Q. What do you look for when hiring a junior analyst/associate?**

A. First and foremost, the ability to assess/judge people is very important. I look for candidates who are perceptive and who do not simply take people at face value. Then I look for the ability to do the financial work, a scientific background, and someone whose personality fits well with the rest of our team.

**Q. What distinguishes a successful venture capitalist from others that are less so?**

A. In the VC world, one is ultimately judged by the deals one does and their returns.

# HOW VENTURE CAPITAL DIRECTORS SPEND THEIR TIME

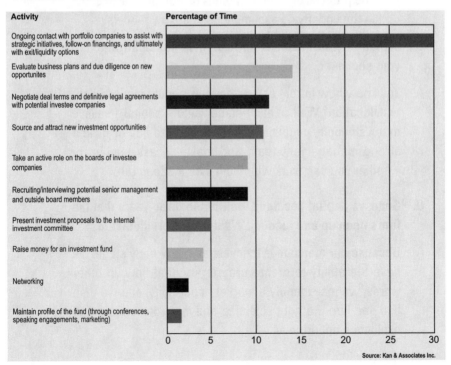

| Activity | Percentage of Time |
| --- | --- |
| Ongoing contact with portfolio companies to assist with strategic initiatives, follow-on financings, and ultimately with exit/liquidity options | |
| Evaluate business plans and due diligence on new opportunites | |
| Negotiate deal terms and definitive legal agreements with potential investee companies | |
| Source and attract new investment opportunities | |
| Take an active role on the boards of investee companies | |
| Recruiting/interviewing potential senior management and outside board members | |
| Present investment proposals to the internal investment committee | |
| Raise money for an investment fund | |
| Networking | |
| Maintain profile of the fund (through conferences, speaking engagements, marketing) | |

Source: Kan & Associates Inc.

**Q. What advice would you give to someone aspiring to land a job at a venture capital firm?**

A. I would tell them that venture capital is not easy to get into, so be patient. Plan A would be to apply to the VC firms. If Plan A fails, consider a Plan B. One good alternative route would be to work at one of the portfolio companies (venture-backed operating companies) as a stepping stone. Then make a point of keeping in touch with the people you contacted at the VC firms and keep the relationships open.

The percentages in the opposite chart tend to change depending on:

- **Stage of the fund.** During the first few years of a fund's "life cycle", the active investment phase, relatively more time is spent on looking for, sourcing, and evaluating new investment opportunities, as well as actually doing the deals. During the middle years of a fund's life, as existing investee companies start to mature, venture capitalists tend to spend relatively more time doing follow-on financings to provide additional funding to portfolio companies. In the later years of a fund's life, as portfolio companies mature and enter the exit phase, more time is spent raising money for a new fund.

- **Stage of the company being invested in.** A VC that invests in early-stage companies spends much more time actively working with the companies. Therefore, a higher percentage of time is spent in ongoing contact with the founders/management teams, recruiting potential senior management, and taking an active role on the boards of investee companies.

- **Stage of the deal.** Although activities like negotiating deal terms/legal agreements and presenting proposals to the internal investment committee may be a small part of time spent during the course of a year, they can consume all of one's time when deals are closing.

- **Size of the VC firm.** Smaller shops may outsource part, or all, of the due diligence function.

- **Type of VC firm.** Independent firms need to raise outside money for their funds, while other firms like the Business Development Bank and some of the bank-owned firms have captive money. So while senior venture capitalists at independent firms can spend a significant amount of their time raising money for a new fund, their counterparts at the bank-owned firms simply go to the investment committee once or twice a quarter for funds. Some labour-sponsored funds have marketing departments to interact with the retail clientele so the investment professional spends less time on fundraising.

- **Record of investment performance.** The length of time required for a fund to raise money also depends on the firm's/partner's track record.

### Profile of the Ideal Venture Capitalist

- ability to network (so being personable and presentable helps)

- ability to assess people

- hands-on industry experience (i.e., project manager)

- tech or biotech savvy

- financial acumen

- good business judgment

- ability to interact with senior executives

### The Top 10 Venture Capital Firms in Canada
### (By number of deals done between 1999 and 2004)

| Investor | # of Companies |
|---|---|
| 1. Fonds de solidarité des travailleurs du Québec (F.T.Q.) | 286 |
| 2. Business Development Bank of Canada (BDC) | 230 |
| 3. CDP Capital – Technology Ventures | 184 |
| 4. Fonds de solidarité (FTQ) | 178 |
| 5. Desjardins Venture Capital | 171 |
| 6. GrowthWorks | 160 |
| 7. Innovatech du Grand Montréal | 158 |
| 8. CDP – Accés Capital | 147 |
| 9. Roynat Capital Inc. | 108 |
| 10. CDP Capital – Amérique | 107 |

*Source: Macdonald & Associates Limited*

### The Top 10 Venture Capital Firms in Canada
### (By dollar volume of deals done between 1999 and 2004)

1. Fonds de solidarité des travailleurs du Québec (F.T.Q.)
2. CDP Capital – Technology Ventures
3. VenGrowth Capital Partners
4. CDP Capital – Communications
5. GrowthWorks

6. Business Development Bank of Canada (BDC)

7. TD Capital

8. RBC Capital Partners

9. Covington Capital Corporation

10. Ventures West Management Inc.

*Source: Macdonald & Associates Limited*

---

## Suggested Reading

1. *Code Name Ginger* (by Steve Kemper, published by Harvard Business School Press)

   This is the story of the Ginger project—the invention of an overly hyped, electric-powered people mover named the Segway Human Transporter. It chronicles the project from conception to manufacture, and allows the reader insights/lessons into the inventor and his high-profile financiers.

2. *Confessions of a Venture Capitalist: Inside the High-Stakes World of Start-up Financing* (by Ruthann Quindlen, published by Warner Business)

   An investment banker turned technology analyst turned venture capitalist shares her experiences in this quasi-"how to" manual for entrepreneurs.

3. *Deal Terms—The Finer Points of Venture Capital Deal Structures, Valuations, Term Sheets, Stock Options and Getting Deals Done* (by Alex Wilmerding, et al., published by Aspatore Books)

Written by a senior venture capitalist, this is a good reference book for understanding various deal structures and terms and how they impact financing decisions.

4. *Done Deals: Venture Capitalists Tell Their Stories* (edited by Udayan Gupta, published by Harvard Business School Press)

Written by a former *Wall Street Journal* writer, this book is a compilation of interviews with 35 of the most prominent venture capitalists in the U.S.

5. *eBoys: The First Inside Account of Venture Capitalists at Work* (by Randall E. Stross, published by Ballantine Books)

A San José State University business history professor tells a story of wealth creation in the Internet era as the partners at Benchmark Capital financed Web-based businesses such as eBay and Priceline.com.

6. *From Concept to Wall Street: A Complete Guide to Entrepreneurship and Venture Capital* (by Oren Fuerst and Uri Geiger, published by Financial Times Prentice Hall)

A comprehensive guide to the entire VC life cycle: planning, funding, managing, and exiting a start-up venture.

7. *Inside the Tornado: Marketing Strategies from Silicon Valley's Cutting Edge* (by Geoffrey A. Moore, published by HarperBusiness)

This best-seller presents the life cycle of technology-based products and explores marketing strategies for each stage.

8. *The Kingmakers: Venture Capital and the Money Behind the Net* (by Karen Southwick, published by John Wiley & Sons)

   The author, executive editor of Forbes, traces the evolution of the VC industry and offers a close-up view of the inner workings of Silicon Valley.

9. *The Money of Invention: How Venture Capital Creates New Wealth* (by Paul A. Gompers and Josh Lerner, published by Harvard Business School Press)

   The authors provide a view of the role venture capital plays in both the economy and an entrepreneur's potential success.

10. *Structuring Venture Capital, Private Equity, and Entrepreneurial Transactions: 2001* (by Jack S. Levin, published by Aspen Publishing)

    Written by a University of Chicago law school professor, this text is a useful reference on the subject.

11. *Taking Research to Market: How to Build and Invest in Successful University Spinouts* (by Kenny Tang, Ajay Vohara, and Roger Freeman, published by Euromoney Books)

    Insights from thirty industry experts should be useful to early stage VCs.

12. *The VC Way: Investment Secrets from the Wizards of Venture Capital* (by Jeffrey Zygmont, published by Perseus Publishing)

    The author lays out venture-investing rules/principles through insights gleaned from interviewing a number of the most successful venture capitalists south of the border.

13. *The Venture Capital Cycle* (by Paul Gompers and Josh Lerner, published by MIT Press)

    Written by two Harvard Business School professors, this research-oriented book walks the reader through the VC business of financing early-stage companies: the raising of funds, how venture capitalists structure a deal to earn their expected return, how investee companies are managed, exit strategy options, etc.

14. *Venture Capital Due Diligence: A Guide to Making Smart Investment Choices and Increasing your Portfolio Returns* (by Justin J. Camp, published by John Wiley & Sons)

    The author, general partner of a Silicon Valley-based seed-stage venture capital firm, shares his personal insights as well as those of several leading venture capitalists in explaining the due diligence process.

15. *Venture Capital Investing: The Complete Handbook for Investing in Private Businesses for Outstanding Profits* (by David Gladstone and Laura Gladstone, published by Financial Times Prentice Hall)

    A seasoned venture capitalist guides readers in terms of doing due diligence on potential VC investments—evaluating the entrepreneurs, the opportunity, the products, etc.

16. *The Ways of the VC* (Inside the Minds Series, published by Aspatore Books)

A contributed volume in which 10 principal/partner-level venture capitalists at the leading American VC firms offer practical advice for the successful financing of start-up companies.

17. *Young Men with Unlimited Capital: The Inside Story of the Legendary Woodstock Festival Told by the Two Who Paid for It* (by Joel Rosenman, John (Peter) Roberts, and Robert H. Pilpel, published by Harcourt Brace Jovanovich)

This book (written by the two young partners of JR Capital) tells the story of how they took out an ad in *The Wall Street Journal* titled "2 Young Men with Unlimited Capital" with the intention of funding good business plans. The men ended up backing Woodstock.

CHAPTER

# Portfolio
# **Manager**

# CHAPTER 8

# Portfolio Manager

## Overview

THE PORTFOLIO MANAGER (PM) ROLE (also known as *money manager, fund manager,* or *investment manager*) is the top of the Bay Street food chain. This is about as good as it gets. A successful portfolio manager with a top-quartile performance record will attract assets to his or her organization, and more assets under management means better compensation (salaries and bonuses for fund managers tend to be positively correlated to the assets under management), better access to company managements, and access to more sell-side firms (the more assets a fund has, the more commissions it has available to pay to brokers). Not to mention the endless courtship by the sell-side for a larger piece of the portfolio manager's commission pie.

The portfolio management (or investment management) function is a straightforward one: To invest other people's money profitably. As well, it is expected that the portfolio outperform either some benchmark index (e.g., S&P/TSX composite, S&P 500, etc.) that reflects the portfolio's mandate or peer group of competitor funds with a similar focus and investment objective. Keep in mind that portfolios can be classified in a number of ways:

1. By asset class: equity (stocks), fixed-income (debt instruments with medium- to long-term maturities), money market (short-term debt instruments), balanced (some combination of equity and debt)

2. By geography: global, regional, country

3. By industry sector: technology, health care, energy, etc.

4. By style: value, growth, momentum, etc.

5. By specialty: emerging markets, etc.

The money that is handed over to a fund manager to invest is typically invested in financial assets (stocks and bonds). How a fund manager then goes about building a diversified portfolio depends on a number of factors, including: the portfolio policy statement and the investment philosophy of the manager.

The portfolio manager job is also considered a second-generation or sometimes third-generation job. Nobody comes straight out of MBA school and lands a role as a professional money manager at an established and respected institution right away. The most common paths to the portfolio manager job are:

1. **Start out on the buy-side as an analyst with coverage responsibilities of 30 to 50 companies across three or four industries.** After a few years, get promoted to a co-manager role on a larger fund or assume portfolio management responsibilities on a smaller fund.

2. **Start out as an equity research associate on the sell-side.** After three years or so, get promoted to a (sell-side) analyst role with primary coverage responsibilities. Then, after demonstrating your analytical and stock-picking abilities to the Street, move to the buy-side as a senior buy-side analyst or money manager.

3. **Start out as an equity research associate on the sell-side.** After three years or so, move over to the buy-side as an analyst providing research and analytical support to the portfolio manager(s). After a few years (typically three to five, although the timing is less defined than it is for a research associate on the sell-side), get promoted to assistant portfolio manager on a larger fund or take on portfolio management responsibilities on a smaller fund.

QUICK FACTS

**EDUCATION**
Bachelor's degree or master's degree in business or economics preferred

**COMPENSATION RANGE**
C$150,000 to multi-millions
Average C$200,000 – $500,000

**INDUSTRY CERTIFICATION**
CFA designation

For the purposes of this chapter, we focus the discussion on managers of actively managed equity funds (versus passive/indexed funds).

### Education

A general business background is generally sufficient for a portfolio manager position, with the exception being an analyst/PM on a life sciences or resource fund where a more technical background would be appropriate. Also, with the recent trend of buy-side firms building/expanding their own investment teams, the ability of a buy-side analyst (the entry-level role on an investment management team) to build financial models has gained importance.

### Compensation

It is accepted wisdom on Bay Street that compensation on the buy-side (with the exception of hedge funds) isn't quite as lucrative as it is on the sell-side. This tends to be true for buy-side analysts and most portfolio managers. However, for the high-profile mutual fund managers with first-quartile performance numbers and billions of dollars under management, or the partners at successful investment counseling firms, the compensation can exceed the seven-figure mark and can be competitive with, or beat, that of the sell-side.

Factors that tend to influence a money manager's total compensation include:

- **Equity ownership.** Senior investment professionals at investment counseling firms participate in the profitability of their firm through equity participation. In a cash flow-rich business, the annual distributions can be meaningful.

- **Experience.** All things being equal, a seasoned analyst or PM will have more leverage in compensation discussions than a lesser experienced colleague.

- **Level of responsibility.** Compensation increases as one moves up the ranks in a money management firm: from investment analyst to senior analyst to co-portfolio manager to lead portfolio manager and for only a few—chief investment officer.

- **Type of institution/employer.** Insurance companies and trust companies tend to pay at the lower end of the range while mutual funds and investment counseling firms pay at the higher end of the range.

- **Portfolio performance.** Most fund managers have a bonus component to their compensation that is based on both short-term performance and intermediate-term performance.

- **Profitability of the firm.** The profitability of the firm is usually driven by two factors: the *size* of the assets (as measured by assets under administration) and the *type* of assets (higher management fees are earned on equity funds than on fixed-income funds).

- **Profitability of the money management group.** At some of the investment management affiliates of the domestic banks, senior investment professionals' bonuses are influenced by the performance of the group as a whole.

- **Discretionary component.** As with most variable/ bonus compensation, there is a discretionary component that reflects the individual's ability to work well with others, etc.

### Industry Certification

Partial or full completion of the CFA program is required to be registered as an investment counselor/portfolio manager (IC/PM) in Canada. If an individual is applying for IC/PM registration to work with a member firm of the Investment Dealers Association (IDA), then an application should be submitted to the IDA. Otherwise, an application should be submitted to the provincial securities regulator. The proficiency requirements of both organizations are similar in that they require applicants to have completed either 1) the Canadian Investment Manager (CIM) program and the first year of the Chartered Financial Analyst (CFA) program, or 2) the Chartered Financial Analyst Program, and to have varying levels of experience as an analyst on either the buy- or sell-side of the Street.

Readers looking for further information on this topic should refer to the section of Part 3 of the OSC's Rules, Policies, & Notices titled Proficiency Requirements for Registrants.

## Investing Styles

- **Momentum.** The focus of momentum investing is price momentum. Momentum investors also seek stocks with the greatest changes in earnings per share growth (on a rolling four-quarter basis) with increasing revenues, and stocks of companies that have a tendency to raise profit forecasts and issue positive earnings surprises. Momentum investors tend to go wherever the money is flowing in.

- **Growth.** Growth managers seek out companies with strong earnings growth prospects and are willing to pay premium multiples for those companies. Proponents of this philosophy tend to be more active in biotech and technology stocks.

- **Value.** Investors with a value orientation typically buy low-multiple (typically out-of-favor) stocks and have a longer-term investment horizon (a buy-and-hold strategy) than those following other investing styles. On one end of the spectrum, there is *absolute* value. These value managers simply buy beaten-down stocks (sometimes disregarding the quality of the company) trading at low multiples (i.e., price-to-book values) if they believe that eventually the value will be realized and the stock will recover. On the other end of the spectrum, there is *relative* value. These value managers look for companies that are cheap relative to their peers. And there are other value practitioners who buy good businesses with competitive advantages for less than they are worth and sell them when they reach their intrinsic value.

- **Growth at a reasonable price (GARP).** A hybrid of the growth and value philosophies, GARP managers look for companies with good business models and that grow at above-average rates compared to the market (the long-term earnings growth rate of the market is in the high single digits), but will not pay much more than the market multiple to own those companies. Some GARP managers have slightly looser criteria and simply look for companies that are attractively valued when compared to their potential growth rate.

- **Sector rotation.** This style is also referred to as market timing. Money managers who invest in this manner look at the economic drivers of a cycle and typically make their sector bets before the stocks in the sector move. For example, a sector rotator may start buying defensive stocks (e.g., consumer staples) at the top of a market cycle in anticipation of, or at the very first signs of, a weakening economy.

- **Socially responsible investing (SRI).** In this style, social values and principles are integrated into the stock selection process. Money managed with an SRI mandate typically screen potential companies/investments against a number of social and environmental criteria. Historically, socially responsible investing simply meant avoiding tobacco, alcohol, gaming, and defense stocks, but now has a broadened mandate to ensure that portfolio companies follow a wide range of socially responsible business practices.

- **Core portfolio strategy.** This strategy focuses on holding quality, liquid, large-cap companies and is often reflective of a blue-chip index. While the investment goal is to beat the benchmark index, this style emphasizes low volatility of returns and preservation of capital. The manager attempts to generate excess returns by varying the weights of each stock holding.

## The Job of Portfolio Construction

The goal of portfolio construction is to create a well-diversified portfolio that offers a combination of capital appreciation potential and dividend income. PMs are required to perform a number of steps when constructing an investment portfolio.

1. **Understand the investment policy statement.** The first consideration of a PM is to understand the investment policy statement for the pool of money being run. The policy statement typically lays out the investment guidelines, such as:

   - overall strategy
   - maximum individual company weights
   - maximum industry weights
   - required industry diversification
   - maximum cash levels
   - use of foreign content and the ability to hedge the foreign exchange exposure
   - use of derivatives
   - use of exchange-traded funds to access industry exposure
   - asset mix

2. **Provide input into the asset allocation decision.** This macro-driven process is typically adjusted on an annual basis and primarily sets the asset mix between different asset classes.

   The following variables are typically taken into consideration: direction of economic growth, monetary policy and interest rates, inflation, valuation, and direction/sentiment of the stock market.

3. **Perform screening and idea generation.** Filtering out what's not relevant is one of the biggest challenges for a money manager. He or she must wade through an endless sea of information in order to find potential stocks to put on the watch list. Money-making investment ideas can be sourced from any number

of sources: the sell-side (salespeople, traders, or analysts), company management teams (who are also in a position to comment on competitors), general reading (financial newspapers, business magazines, industry journals, etc.), or simply one's understanding of the economic/market cycle.

4. **Undertake the fundamental research process.** The process of developing an in-depth understanding of a company and its industry begins with reading. Portfolios managers can access sell-side research, annual reports (10Ks), and quarterly reports (10Qs), and listen to recent company conference calls. The due diligence process continues as the fund manager seeks out the sell-side analysts that know the story best. Most PMs tend to have a few select go-to analysts for each industry sector.

   Ideally, the portfolio manager then interviews company management. If the PM's firm has enough influence (meaning it has enough assets to make it a potentially large shareholder), the PM can call the company and arrange a one-on-one meeting with senior management. If the firm is not large enough, the PM may go to the broker who has the best relationship with the company and ask that broker to set up a meeting.

5. **Determine the value of the company and its securities.** The PM will now perform financial analysis (e.g., traditional multiple analysis, discounted cash flow analysis, dividend yield calculation, net asset value calculation, comparative company valuations, etc.) on the company in accordance with his or her own style.

6. **Determine the appropriate weighting (in terms of industry exposure and the overall portfolio) given the return potential and risk profile of the company.**

Given that the preservation of capital is a key objective of the portfolio management function, the job of assessing risk is one of the most important elements in the process. Then accumulate a position. This may mean buying a starting position immediately or, in the case of a value manager, may involve waiting for the stock to trade at the right (lower) price.

7. **Monitor portfolio and markets.** This is an ongoing rebalancing process, as the portfolio manager monitors macroeconomic and capital market conditions/trends to assess their impact on portfolio holdings and companies on the watch list. Individual holdings are re-evaluated if the company fundamentals change or if the stock price reaches its target price.

8. **Measure and analyze investment performance.** This is typically done in a regular (quarterly) investment performance meeting. Returns are analyzed to determine which sector bets and individual positions added value.

"Think for yourself, be patient and wait for good opportunities, focus on risk, and don't pay too much for a stock."
—*John Smolinski, CFA, Portfolio Manager,*
*TD Asset Management*

## A Day in the Life of a Top Portfolio Manager

**David Vanderwood**, CFA, is senior vice president at Burgundy Asset Management. He has more than 10 years of experience in the investment business and was most recently an analyst at Odlum Brown, researching both Canadian and U.S. equities.

Bachelor of Commerce from University of British Columbia, 1993

I bought my first stock when I was 12 years old. At a young age, I was fascinated by investing. Then for some reason I lost interest for awhile—it may have had something to do with hitting puberty—so my first year at the University of British Columbia was in sciences. After that first year, I left university and worked for two years. It was during that time that I picked up a copy of *Fortune* magazine and read an article on risk versus reward. I was instantly hooked on investing, so I went back to UBC and enrolled in the commerce program. I did not miss a single day of school over the next four years.

At the end of my second year, I applied for, and was accepted into, the Portfolio Management Foundation program. The PMF program is a two-year extra-curricular program for a select group of commerce students in years three and four of their coursework. The students (designated as research associates in year three and fund managers in year four) get to manage a real portfolio valued at approximately $2.5 million. Once accepted into the PMF program, the other research associates and I spent our next two summers in Toronto, Vancouver, or New York City doing an internship at a participating firm on either the buy or sell-side of the Street. Throughout the summer we also attended investment seminars hosted/led by mentors of our program. During the school year, we met regularly, and under the guidance of local mentors we made investment decisions for the portfolio. The program was an extremely good learning experience for me—it was like putting the test before the lesson—and paved the way for my career in this business.

After graduation, I went to work for a successful venture capitalist named Richard Bonnycastle who ran Cavendish Investing in Alberta. There was little status in going to work for a small investment shop in Alberta but I knew I could learn a lot from Richard. I also knew that if I could learn to invest properly, I could write my own ticket one day. After my first year as an analyst, I was given a fund to run.

While at Cavendish, I met Murray Leith Jr. We became friends and often exchanged investment ideas. I felt that Murray was a talented and driven individual, and a smart investor. I felt that I could learn from him and that working for him could take me to the next level in terms of my investing knowledge. So, after four good years at Cavendish, I went to work with Murray at Odlum Brown as an analyst.

In my quest to work with the best and smartest people, after four years at Odlum Brown I joined Burgundy Asset Management to work with Allan MacDonald and Richard Rooney. We buy good companies cheap, typically at a 30% discount to what we believe they're worth. We sell companies when they become expensive, when they reach their intrinsic value. Our cash position is the end result of these individual decisions—it's not a call on the market. And just to clarify, we don't buy stocks just because they're cheap. We buy good companies with competitive advantages and sustainable franchises that make good returns but are out-of-favour in the market.

Here's what a typical day might look like:

**7:00 a.m.**  Get on the subway. Read the business section of the *National Post.*

**7:30 a.m.**  Get into the office. Check my e-mails.

**8:00 a.m.**  Weekly (internal) management meeting starts. It is attended by the senior staffers of the firm, including other portfolio managers, the head of marketing, the head of operations, and our CFO. The meeting starts off with the portfolio managers providing an overview of the markets and our current investment thinking. It is necessary to keep our marketing people in the loop in terms of our investment views since, as a firm with high-net-worth clients, the portfolio managers have little or no client contact. We also discuss operational issues, such as our plans to expand the office, and administrative issues, such as co-ordinating the portfolio managers' schedules to accommodate the interview process of a potential young analyst.

**9:00 a.m.**    Company ABC's conference call to discuss quarter-end results begins.

**10:00 a.m.**    Management of heavy equipment auctioneer company XYZ, along with the institutional salesperson that set up the meeting, arrive at my firm's reception area. My analyst sits in on the meeting. It turns out that this company is the industry leader in terms of gross auction sales, but has only 1% market share in a high-margin business line—used equipment trading. There seems to be a lot of room for growth. In the course of the conversation, the management team mentions a formidable competitor south of the border.

**10:55 a.m.**    My analyst and I review our notes of the meeting. I ask him to do further work on both the company we just met and its U.S. counterpart.

**11:10 a.m.**    Call CFO of company BCD to compare notes on our assumptions behind the company's sales forecasts and profit margins. Based on our conversation, I tweak my financial models for the company.

**11:50 a.m.**    Head down to the food court to grab a sandwich.

**12:20 p.m.**    Back at my desk. Eat lunch and get caught up on my reading: today's business section of *The Globe and Mail*, and the current issues of *Forbes*, *Fortune* and *BusinessWeek*.

**2:00 p.m.**     Management of company STU arrives. The CFO happens to be a former sell-side analyst whose former employer we did a lot of business with. So, we take a few minutes to exchange industry scuttlebutt and get caught up before launching into a full discussion of the company's business prospects.

**3:00 p.m.**     Biweekly (internal) investment meeting starts. This is an informal session during which the team can bounce ideas around. One of my colleagues raises some concerns about how proposed legislation may negatively affect some of our holdings. Then we listen to a couple of new investment ideas proposed by our younger analysts.

**5:00 p.m.**     One of the companies in my portfolio has just reported after the market close, so I dial into the conference call.

**5:50 p.m.**     Check my voicemails. There are a number of messages from sell-side analysts and institutional salespeople. I only have time to return one, so I call the analyst who is the only bear on the Street on my largest holding.

**6:00 p.m.**     A prospective job candidate shows up for our scheduled interview. We talk about her education, her work experience, and her life experience. I'm impressed—she's smart, driven, and has a level of maturity beyond her years. She seems obsessed with investing. She's done a lot of investment reading outside of her CFA studies. I want her to meet my partners.

**6:30 p.m.**     Grab the business section of the *Financial Times* to read on the subway ride home.

**8:30 p.m.**     Put the kids to bed.

**8:45 p.m.**     Sit down to update several of my spreadsheet models.

**10:30 p.m.**   Call it a night.

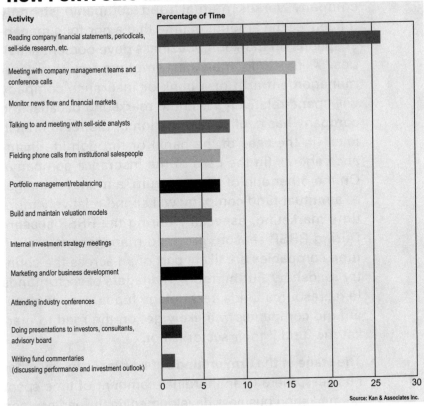

# HOW PORTFOLIO MANAGERS SPEND THEIR TIME

| Activity | Percentage of Time |
| --- | --- |
| Reading company financial statements, periodicals, sell-side research, etc. | |
| Meeting with company management teams and conference calls | |
| Monitor news flow and financial markets | |
| Talking to and meeting with sell-side analysts | |
| Fielding phone calls from institutional salespeople | |
| Portfolio management/rebalancing | |
| Build and maintain valuation models | |
| Internal investment strategy meetings | |
| Marketing and/or business development | |
| Attending industry conferences | |
| Doing presentations to investors, consultants, advisory board | |
| Writing fund commentaries (discussing performance and investment outlook) | |

Source: Kan & Associates Inc.

The above percentages tend to change depending on:

- **The size of the investment department or firm.** The size of the investment department or firm determines the resources that can be dedicated to the process of stock analysis and selection. Therefore, portfolio managers with larger investment teams have the luxury of delegating primary research functions, such as financial modeling, to their analysts, while money managers at smaller firms either do it themselves or not at all (and rely more on the sell-side for primary research).

- **The type of money management firm.** The *type* of firm (investment management arm of a domestic bank versus investment department of an insurance company versus mutual fund company) strongly influences the amount of time that a portfolio manager spends on marketing/business development activities. A portfolio manager employed at the asset management arm of a bank or insurance company will spend relatively less time marketing because the company has captive distribution at the retail branch level (in the case of the bank) or through life insurance agents (in the case of the insurance company). On the other end of the spectrum, a money manager at a mutual fund company will spend relatively more time marketing, especially during the RRSP season. During RRSP season, portfolio managers at mutual fund companies are likely part of an across-the-country roadshow. Furthermore, managers of sector funds (e.g., resource funds, technology funds, etc.) at mutual fund companies will likely get on the road to market the fund if their sector is hot.

- **The stage of the firm or fund's life cycle.** As in any other business, there is an inordinate amount of time spent on marketing/business development in the earlier stage of a firm or fund. For example, a portfolio manager of a start-up investment counsel firm may allocate his or her time as follows: one-third on marketing/business development, one-third on stock selection and portfolio management, and one-third on managing client relationships. Business development can take both active forms (e.g., running investment seminars) and passive forms (e.g., community involvement as a board member of a local hospital or charity). Once the target level of assets is reached, the time devoted to new business development falls off noticeably.

- **The investment style.** Fund managers with a value focus (implying a longer-term investment horizon) spend relatively less time on monitoring the daily gyrations of the market and talking to institutional salespeople. Alternatively, they spend more time doing fundamental research, reading company financial statements, and meeting with company management teams. The opposite would be true for a momentum investor.

- **The size of the portfolio or firm.** The more assets that a fund company has under management, the higher the likelihood that the fund could be a major shareholder in any company. Corporate management teams recognize this and therefore are more likely to grant one-on-one meetings with senior members of the management team to portfolio managers at larger funds than they would to smaller funds.

- **The proportion of U.S. versus Canadian names in the fund manager's universe.** There is a smaller universe of publicly listed Canadian companies. Therefore, managers with a Canadian-only mandate will spend relatively more time simply updating their knowledge on companies they already know. Managers with a U.S. mandate spend relatively more time learning new names than do their counterparts with a Canadian-only mandate.

- **Seniority of the fund manager.** Senior fund managers will likely know the history, products, management, and margin profile of many of the companies and industries he or she tends to invest in, and will spend a lot of time monitoring the companies and waiting for a catalyst before buying or selling the stock. Analysts and junior portfolio managers, on the other hand, tend to spend more of their time learning about industries and companies.

- **The commission volume.** The amount of commission a firm pays to the sell-side of the Street affects its access to, and relationships with, the sell-side.

Portfolio managers that generate a lot of trading commissions, by virtue of having either lots of assets or high turnover of their portfolio, will naturally get preferential treatment by the sell-side, such as access to one-on-one meetings with analysts and being the brokers' first call on trade ideas or deal allocations.

## A Chat with a Portfolio Manager

**Keith Graham**, CFA, is senior vice president and portfolio manager at AGF Management. Prior to joining AGF, he was a portfolio manager at AIM Trimark, where he managed a multi-billion-dollar flagship fund and was the recipient of several coveted industry awards. Keith won both the Best Canadian Balanced Fund award and the Best Canadian Small Cap Fund award at the 2001 Canadian Investment Awards. He then won the Best Canadian Balanced Fund award again in 2002.

Q. **When did you first realize that you wanted to be in the investment management business?**

A. When I was in my late teens, I knew I wanted to be an investor. I knew I wanted to be a portfolio manager. I remember that when I was doing my undergraduate degree at the University of Western Ontario, I picked up a copy of *Fortune* magazine that made a strong impression on me—it showed Jim Craig, the founder of U.S. mutual fund heavyweight Janus Capital, sitting in a hot tub in the Rockies. It seemed that a career in money management had all the right ingredients: It was intellectually stimulating, you could make a lot of money, and you could live wherever you want. I wanted in! So while still in undergraduate studies, I enrolled in the Canadian Securities Course. I also did a lot of investment reading—books like *The Intelligent Investor*, *A Random Walk Down Wall Street*, *Common Stocks and Uncommon Profits*, and Ben Graham's *Security Analysis*. I also read a number of Berkshire Hathaway's annual reports. I was intent on forming my own investment thinking.

**Q. How did you get your start in the business?**

A. After graduating from my undergraduate studies, I went to work for Fidelity Investments. I started out in the call centre and worked my way up to managing a retail branch in Baltimore. I enjoyed it, and was making good money, but it wasn't what I wanted to do. So I returned to Canada and went back to Western for an MBA. In my second year at Western, the Active Equities group at the Ontario Teachers' Pension Plan Board came to campus to recruit an investment analyst. I went through the interview process and got hired. They offered me a salary of $50,000, which was one of the lower starting salaries offered to anyone in my graduating class, but the money was secondary since I finally got a chance to do what I really wanted to do.

**Q. I imagine that working at Ontario Teachers' must have been a good learning experience. As I understand it, Ontario Teachers' succeeded Confederation Life as the training ground for talent on the buy-side.**

A. Yes, it was a very good learning experience. I was lucky— there aren't too many firms or people that really take the time to train young analysts. And coincidently, the lead portfolio manager at Teachers' at the time was formerly a PM at Confed Life, so she brought over the Confed model for analyzing companies.

**Q. Did you take away any lessons from that experience?**

A. Yes, there were three. First, I learned that investing, and the business of evaluating companies, is a disciplined process. One must take the time to go through that process: Figure out what it is that a company does; who its competitors are; the profit margins, the capital intensity, and the cash flow characteristics; the historical financial performance; and the proper valuation metrics for the industry. Second, I learned to focus on the long term. Third, I realized the benefits of working with a good team.

**Q. What's the biggest challenge for a money manager?**

A. With all the information coming at us, it can be a challenge trying to wade through all the noise in order to get to the relevant information. It can also be a challenge maintaining one's patience and continuing to focus on the long term in a short-term world.

**Q. What characteristics does a successful money manager have?**

A. First and foremost, the ability to evaluate and value a business is crucial. It is also important to be an independent thinker and have a long-term perspective. Having discipline and the strength of one's convictions also plays a role. Finally, the ability to prioritize—knowing what's important— is very important. Here I don't mean just from a business perspective, but from a life perspective as well. Being able to balance work and family/friends is part of being successful.

**Q. What do you look for when hiring an analyst?**

A. I look for five things:

1. A passion for investing. I like to see that a candidate has done investment reading outside of their university or CFA studies.

2. An independent thinker. During the interview process, I listen for clues.

3. Intellect and smarts. I look for good common sense.

4. Academic credentials. Ideally, I look for an MBA, CFA, or CA.

5. People skills. I look for good people who are personable and that I want to be partners with. Furthermore, the people skills will be a necessity when interviewing management teams, talking to suppliers and customers, etc. People will likely be more open and helpful if they're dealing with people they like.

**Q. What advice would you give to someone trying to land a job on the buy-side?**

A. Take the time to understand what investing is. Understand the different investment philosophies. Then understand who you are and how you think, and which investment style fits your personality and temperament the best. This will allow you to target your job search to those investment firms that fit best with your style. And keep in mind that plum jobs don't open up that often, so be persistent and keep in touch with people that you've interviewed with.

In addition, I would suggest writing up a sample research report on a publicly traded company. This accomplishes several things: First, it demonstrates your commitment to getting into the investment management business (as opposed to it being one of several jobs/industries you're applying to just to get a job). Second, it gives the interviewer a sense of how far along your investment knowledge is relative to your peers. Sure, every job candidate that walks through our doors knows about buying low and selling high. And sure, every candidate has heard of Warren Buffett, but I (and other portfolio managers in a hiring capacity) would like to see that, at some basic level, you can analyze and value a company based on sound investment principles. Third, if you find yourself thoroughly enjoying the investment analysis process while you're working on the report, then you know this business is for you.

## Some Practical Job Considerations

1. **Working for a small money management firm versus a large one.**

   An advantage of working at a small money management firm is that it could be a good training ground. For example, with a small team of only three professionals (one PM and two analysts), the less senior analyst will likely be given the responsibility for trading the equity and fixed income securities in the portfolios, enabling more market perspective. The senior analyst may receive portfolio management responsibilities (e.g., managing a small-cap fund) sooner than they would at a larger institution. The training at a small firm tends to develop good generalists.

   Another advantage of working at a small shop is the ability to invest in smaller-cap companies and acquire/exit positions quicker. The following example illustrates the point:

   *Assumptions:*

   • Money manager A has $1 billion in AUM.

   • Money manager B has $5 billion in AUM.

   • Both managers have an average holding/position size of 200 basis points (two percent) of AUM.

   Therefore,

   • Manager A would need to invest $20 million for a full position, whereas

   • Manager B would need to invest $100 million for a full position

   Assume that company XYZ stock has a market capitalization of $1 billion.

- Manager A would own 2.0% of the company for a full position.

- Manager B would own 10.0% of the company for a full position.

Liquidity—getting in and out of a stock with minimal impact—is less of a concern for manager A, whose holding of company XYZ stock is only two percent. Also, manager A is likely to acquire positions quicker, ideally before the stock moves.

A disadvantage of working for a small firm, assuming a smaller firm has less commissions to pay the sell-side, is less service from the sell-side and less one-on-one meetings with analysts.

Another disadvantage of working for a small firm is less access to company management. Companies are not as responsive to requests for meetings when a money manager is not seen as a potential large institutional shareholder.

Naturally, the above advantages and disadvantages of working for a small fund would be the opposite of the advantages and disadvantages of working for a large fund, with the exception of the first point. It can also be an advantage to work at a large firm from a training ground perspective, since the investment team is supported by more infrastructure and is exposed to more deal flow, more information flow, etc.

2. **The type of institution may not allow the portfolio much flexibility in terms of money management style.**

Typically, if the money in the fund is private money (money in the corporate account or the employee pension fund), the lead manager may have some discretion as to how closely he or she sticks to the philosophy. It is conceivable that a senior analyst gets promoted into a portfolio manager role where the investment philosophy of the firm traditionally has had a strong value bias, but over time the new manager imposes his or her own value-with-growth orientation to the portfolio. The bottom line is this: As long as the performance is good, a money manager running private money has some discretion as to the investment philosophy/style he or she wishes to adopt.

On the other hand, if a portfolio manager is running mutual fund money, there tends to be less discretion. Mutual fund companies usually offer a variety of fund products with defined product offerings (value funds, growth funds, etc.). The portfolio manager is then constrained by the style of the funds because of unitholder expectations and the specific mandate of the fund.

3. **Those interested in the portfolio manager function should also consider the venture capitalist role (chapter 7).**

   Although both the portfolio manager and venture capitalist manage a portfolio of securities, the primary difference is that the VC deals with early-stage private companies, whereas the PM deals primarily with public companies. That difference aside, the similarities are many:

   a. Both have the challenge of sifting through a lot of information to find a few good investment ideas. For the VC, this is in the form of business plans submitted by entrepreneurs. For the PM, this is in the form of sell-side research and the financial statements of publicly traded companies.

b. Both are trying to earn a consistently superior rate of return of their portfolios.

c. Compensation for both tends to be tied to bottom-line performance of their funds. Performance is measured one of two ways:

- Relative performance is the performance/ track record of a portfolio manager relative to a benchmark index (e.g., S&P 500 index) or peer group of competitor funds with a similar focus and investment objective. Typically, a manager's performance is discussed in terms of underperformance or outperformance of a relevant market index by "x" number of basis points, or by the fund's ranking against its peer group expressed relative to quartile standing (e.g., a fund may be a first-quartile performer). In the relative performance game, a fund manager has done his or her job well if he or she delivers a portfolio return of 13% in a given time frame when the benchmark index was up 10%. Conversely, if the market index was down 10% and a fund manager was only down 7%, he or she looks like a hero. Institutional clients (i.e., pension funds and endowment funds) tend to judge managers on relative performance.

- Absolute performance, on the other hand, is the focus of the client on the absolute performance numbers. Retail and high-net-worth clients tend to judge managers on absolute performance.

4. **The true money manager responsibilities, which have been the focus of this chapter, are not part of the portfolio manager function at certain financial institutions.**

   In these cases, the portfolio manager title is given to individuals located "in the field" (e.g., within the retail branch network) who act as financial advisors/account managers, and the job is much more geared to client service then stock selection. In many instances, these portfolio managers determine the individuals' investment objectives and risk tolerances and simply match the individual to some model portfolio. On occasion, adjustments to the model portfolio must be made. For example, oil and gas executives probably don't want more exposure to energy in their personal stock portfolios.

5. **In the money management business, the focus is on the portfolio performance.**

   A portfolio manager who underperforms two years in a row should probably be concerned about their job security.

"You've got to enjoy what you're doing. Due to the focus in this industry on bottom line performance, there is a lot of pressure and stress. Having a genuine passion for the business and being confident in your own work helps in dealing with the stress."

—*Wally Kusters, CFA, Portfolio Manager,*
*Barrantagh Investment Management*

## The 20 Largest Mutual Fund Companies in 2003

| Company | Assets ($000s) |
|---------|---------------:|
| 1. RBC Asset Management Inc. | 43,860,616 |
| 2. Investors Group Inc. | 43,084,510 |
| 3. CIBC Asset Management Inc. | 40,543,940 |
| 4. AIM Trimark Investments | 40,344,293 |
| 5. Mackenzie Financial Corp. | 35,363,502 |
| 6. TD Asset Management Inc. | 33,768,629 |
| 7. C.I. Mutual Funds Inc. | 33,474,725 |
| 8. Fidelity Investments Canada Ltd. | 31,863,108 |
| 9. AGF Management Ltd. | 25,127,957 |
| 10. Franklin Templeton Investments | 19,540,323 |
| 11. BMO Investments Inc. | 17,598,489 |
| 12. Scotia Securities Inc. | 13,615,481 |
| 13. AIC Ltd. | 12,815,518 |
| 14. Phillips Hager & North Ltd. | 11,768,628 |
| 15. Dynamic Mutual Funds | 9,885,590 |
| 16. National Bank Mutual Funds | 5,788,415 |
| 17. Fiducie Desjardins | 4,733,925 |
| 18. Altamira Investment Services Inc. | 4,318,125 |
| 19. Guardian Group of Funds Ltd. | 3,877,193 |
| 20. Manulife Investments | 3,792,907 |

Source: *National Post*

## The 12 Largest Public-Sector Pension Funds

| Company | Assets (in Millions of Dollars) |
|---|---:|
| 1. Caisse de Depot et placement du Quebec | 118,838 |
| 2. Ontario Teachers' Pension Plan | 75,700 |
| 3. Canada Pension Plan | 51,925 |
| 4. OMERS | 32,709 |
| 5. Quebec Government & Public Employees' Retirement Plan | 30,997 |
| 6. Hospitals of Ontario Pension Plan | 18,657 |
| 7. BC Municipal Pension Plan | 16,517 |
| 8. Quebec Pension Plan | 15,889 |
| 9. Ontario Pension Board | 12,275 |
| 10. BC Teachers' Pension Plan | 11,484 |
| 11. BC Public Service Pension Plan | 10,867 |
| 12. Alberta Local Authorities Pension Plan | 9,655 |

Source: *National Post*

## The Largest Life Insurance Companies in 2003

| Company | Revenues ($000s) |
|---|---|
| 1. Sun Life Financial Inc. | 22,056,000 |
| 2. Manulife Financial Corp. | 16,656,000 |
| 3. Great-West Lifeco Inc. | 13,429,000 |
| 4. Industrial Alliance Insurance and Financial Services Inc. | 3,351,700 |
| 5. The Maritime Life Assurance Co. | 3,017,487 |
| 6. Desjardins Financial Security Life Assurance Inc. | 2,159,668 |
| 7. Northbridge Financial Corp. | 1,162,369 |
| 8. SSQ, Life Insurance Co. Inc. | 873,130 |
| 9. Transamerica Life Canada | 839,144 |
| 10. The Independent Order of Foresters | 703,550 |
| 11. The Empire Life Insurance Co. | 668,889 |
| 12. UnumProvident Corp. | 630,811 |

Source: *National Post*

## Suggested Reading

1. *Applied Equity Analysis: Stock Valuation Techniques for Wall Street Professionals* (by James English, published by McGraw-Hill)

   Written by an equity analyst with 20 years of experience at JP Morgan, this book takes the reader through the entire valuation process, from financial statement analysis through to the final investment recommendation.

2. *Beating the Street* (by Peter Lynch, published by Simon & Schuster)

   Peter Lynch, using his common-sense approach to investing, continues to give the average investor insights and guidance on how to beat the pros.

3. *Buffettology: The Previously Unexplained Techniques That Have Made Warren Buffett the World's Most Famous Investor* (by Mary Buffett and David Clark, published by Simon & Schuster)

   This book, written by Buffett's former daughter-in-law, guides the reader through his key investment concepts: buying a share in a business, identifying excellent businesses, waiting for the perfect pitch, etc.

4. *The Buffettology Workbook: Value Investing the Warren Buffett Way* (by Mary Buffett and David Clark, published by Scribner)

   A step-by-step guide to identifying and evaluating potential investments using Buffett's principles.

5. *Classics: An Investor's Anthology* (by Charles Ellis and James Vertin, published by McGraw-Hill)

   A collection of investment writings by the most successful investors over the last century.

6. *Common Stocks and Uncommon Profits and Other Writings* (by Philip Fisher and Kenneth Fisher, published by John Wiley & Sons)

   Written by one of the pioneers of modern investment theory.

7. *Damodaran on Valuation: Security Analysis for Investment and Corporate Finance* (by Aswath Damodaran, published by John Wiley & Sons)

An NYU Stern Business School finance professor provides a good overview of three valuation approaches for investment analysis: discounted cash flow, relative valuation, and contingent claim valuation.

8. *The Essays of Warren Buffett: Lessons for Corporate America* (by Warren Buffett and Lawrence Cunningham, published by The Cunningham Group)

Lawrence Cunningham has selected lessons from Buffett's annual letters to the shareholders of Berkshire Hathaway, written over the past few decades, and arranged them into a thematically organized work.

9. *Financial Statement Analysis: A Practitioner's Guide* (by Martin Fridson and Fernando Alvarez, published by John Wiley & Sons)

This is a practical guide for understanding and interpreting financial statements and reports. The author's use of real-world examples and conversational tone makes it an easier read than most finance texts.

10. *Integrated Wealth Management: The New Direction for Portfolio Managers* (by Jean Brunel, published by Institutional Investor Books)

The author, formerly chief investment officer of JP Morgan's Global Private Bank and of U.S. Bancorp's

Private Asset Management Group, addresses wealth management issues for high-net-worth port-folio managers (as distinct from institutional money managers).

11. *The Intelligent Investor* (by Benjamin Graham, pub-lished by Harper and Row)

    Benjamin Graham's classic text on value investing embodies the sound principles and investment philosophies that have produced other investment greats such as Warren Buffett.

12. *Investment Philosophies: Successful Investment Philosophies and the Greatest Investors that Made them Work* (by Aswath Damodaran, published by John Wiley & Sons)

    An NYU Stern Business School finance professor offers an academic assessment of a number of investment philosophies and strategies.

13. *The Money Masters* (by John Train, published by Harper & Row)

    John Train, a seasoned portfolio manager and financial columnist, interviews nine of the most successful investors of the previous generation, including Warren Buffett, Ben Graham, and John Templeton, and effectively encapsulates their investing philosophies.

14. *The Mutual Fund Business* (by Robert Pozen, pub-lished by MIT Press)

    Written by the former vice chairman of Fidelity Investments, this book provides a comprehensive overview of the mutual fund industry as a business—

from the structure of the industry and operations of the companies, to the various investment strategies.

15. *The New Money Masters* (by John Train, published by Harper Perennial)

John Train follows up his bestselling *The Money Masters* with interviews of great investors such as Peter Lynch, Jim Rogers, and George Soros who came to prominence in the 1980s.

16. *One Up on Wall Street: How to Use What You Already Know to Make Money in the Market* (by Peter Lynch, published by Simon & Schuster)

Peter Lynch, formerly the star manager of Fidelity's successful flagship Magellan Fund (the largest equity fund in the U.S. at the time), encourages amateur investors to seek out investment opportunities in easy-to-understand companies that they encounter in their everyday lives.

17. *Security Analysis: Principles and Technique* (by Benjamin Graham and David L. Dodd, published by McGraw-Hill)

Originally published in 1934, this book by Benjamin Graham and David Dodd continues to be regarded as a classic text on fundamental security analysis.

18. *The Warren Buffett Portfolio: Mastering the Power of the Focus Investment Strategy* (by Robert Hagstrom, published by John Wiley & Sons)

Buffett's idea that "knowledge decreases risk, not the number of stocks in your portfolio" is a core theme of this book. The author espouses a long-term (five years plus), focused approach (a relatively concentrated portfolio of no more than 15 good businesses/stocks) to building a portfolio.

19. *The Warren Buffett Way: Investment Strategies of the World's Greatest Investor* (by Robert Hagstrom, published by John Wiley & Sons)

An overview of Warren Buffett's investment philosophy and an analysis of his past investments in an effort to teach the reader how Buffett selects individual companies.

CHAPTER

# Hedge Fund
# MANAGER

# CHAPTER 9

# Hedge Fund Manager

## Overview

THE WORD IS OUT. Hedge funds have become the new, new thing (and the employer of choice for many) in the Canadian securities industry. The unlimited financial upside, the attractiveness of building one's own business, and being on the cutting edge of a new trend in the Canadian financial services industry—these are just a few of the reasons hedge funds have managed to lure away some of Bay Street's best traders, analysts, and money managers.

Entrepreneurship and innovation aside, most would argue that it's about the money. Think about it—some of the Street's top talent up and left their managing director titles and their seven-figure paycheques to start their own funds. They certainly didn't do that to earn *less*.

In reference to this phenomenon on Wall Street, U.S. Securities and Exchange Commission Chairman William H. Donaldson remarked, "They are a brain drain on Wall Street."

The lure of Bay Street has always been the huge financial upside in the pay-for-performance culture. Whether you were in sales, trading, research, or investment banking, if you brought in the business, you were compensated generously for your efforts. And philosophically, there was no cap in terms of what one could earn. That all started to change in 1987, however, when the Canadian chartered banks were allowed to own brokerage firms. The country's biggest brokers were then bought by the banks. A decade later, the most successful independent firms were acquired by banks as well (Gordon Capital by HSBC Securities and First Marathon by National Bank Financial). And while compensation levels have remained lofty by Main Street standards, compensation went from direct-drive compensation formulas (where producers are paid a direct percentage of the revenues they bring to their firms) to more subjective bonus pool formulas, and the Street witnessed a tempering of compensation levels. As one trader employed at a bank-owned dealer aptly put it, "They (the firm) didn't go to a (bonus) pool system to pay us *more*."

So where does the top, seasoned talent on the Street go to ply their trade if they want to make the most of their peak earning years? They essentially have two choices:

1. **The partner-owned institutional equity boutiques**. These are successful partnerships that tend to hire big producers with the promise of more direct-drive compensation formulas and equity ownership. In the 1980s, it was firms like First Marathon, Gordon Capital, and Loewen, Ondaatje, McCutcheon (LOM). A decade later, it was firms like Newcrest and Griffiths McBurney & Partners (GMP).

   In the old First Marathon days, the institutional salespeople would get a commission of 16% of their agency commissions. And pre-Spitzer and the global settlement, analysts could earn generous finder's fees (typically 10% of the I-banking fees) for bringing in investment banking deals.

   Now, top analysts and institutional salespeople are making about $1 million a year and top traders are making approximately $1.5 million a year. Not a bad living. But what if you're *really* good and you want to make more— like lots more? And you no longer want someone else to decide your bonus? Then you seriously consider option 2.

2. **Start (or join) a hedge fund.**

### Education

There are primarily three functional roles within a hedge fund: portfolio manager, investment analyst, and trader. Portfolio managers and traders that join (or start up) hedge funds tend to be seasoned, proven professionals so educational background at that level is secondary. For the analyst role, having a finance degree would be a definite asset.

### Compensation

The compensation range of senior professionals on the buy-side tends to be lower than that of the sell-side (with the exception of high-profile mutual fund managers with good performance numbers and billions of dollars under management, or the partners at successful investment counseling firms). Another exception would be the senior hedge fund managers, analysts, and traders. The reason for this is the performance-based incentive fee structure of hedge funds that allows its partners to participate in the returns it generates for its clients. The section titled "Why Start (or Work For) a Hedge Fund" goes into further detail about the economics of working at a hedge fund.

**QUICK FACTS**

**EDUCATION**
Undergraduate and/or postgraduate studies in business or economics

**COMPENSATION RANGE**
Hedge fund manager:
$100,000 to multi-millions

Hedge fund analyst
$100,000 – $700,000

**INDUSTRY CERTIFICATION**
CFA designation required

### Industry Certification

Partial or full completion of the CFA program is required to be registered as an investment counselor/portfolio manager (IC/PM) in Canada. If an individual is applying for IC/PM registration to work with a hedge fund, an application should be submitted to the provincial securities regulator. Applicants are required to have completed either 1) the Canadian Investment Manager (CIM) program and the first year of the Chartered Financial Analyst (CFA) program, or 2) the Chartered Financial Analyst Program, and to have varying levels of experience as an analyst on either the buy- or sell-side of the Street.

## So What Are Hedge Funds?

Hedge funds are specialized money management firms or investment structures/vehicles that employ alternative investment strategies in managing a private commingled investment pool.

Hedge funds are typically set up as limited partnerships where the manager of the fund is the general partner and the investors are the limited partners.

Because the limited partnership interests are not offered to the public, hedge funds are exempted from securities registration and do not have to report their performance or asset information to anyone other than the limited partners. (This is in contrast to the traditional mutual fund industry, which must disclose its information to the public.) The lack of publicly available information, together with the large minimum investment requirements, has given hedge funds an aura of exclusivity.

Hedge funds have, until recently through some retail products, been primarily marketed to "accredited" investors. These are effectively affluent individuals defined as:

a. an individual with a liquid net worth exceeding $1 million, or

b. an individual with net income before taxes exceeding $200,000 (or $300,00 if combined with that of a spouse).

## Why Invest in Hedge Funds

Hedge funds are arguably the most expensive form of discretionary money management there is, but the merits of this type of investment vehicle outweigh the incremental cost. With the falling stock markets over the past few years, investors have looked to non-conventional asset classes to provide downside protection against further market declines. The appeal of absolute returns in all market conditions, with lower levels of risk than most traditional asset classes, has attracted both individual and institutional money. In Warren Buffett's words, "Hedge funds have become the latest holy grail."

A few reasons to invest in hedge funds include:

1. **The potential for positive returns regardless of market direction.** Whereas the traditional money management industry works to post strong relative returns and therefore aims to outperform a market index, the goal of hedge funds is to deliver absolute returns within a certain range (typically high single digits or low double digits per year) irrespective of the market performance.

   So if the TSX/S&P is expected to be up 20% in a given year, mutual fund manager A is looking to beat 20%. If the TSX/S&P is expected to be down 20%, mutual fund manager A would be doing a good job if he or she was down 19.9% or less.

   Not so with hedge fund managers. Hedge fund manager X is expected to deliver positive returns regardless of whether the broad market was up or down.

2. **Low variability of returns.** The goal of hedge fund managers is to generate consistent positive returns with low levels of volatility.

3. **Diversification.** Returns are uncorrelated with equities and other traditional asset classes.

4. **The hedge fund manager's interests are aligned with those of the investors.** Typically, a significant amount of the manager's liquid net worth is invested alongside that of the investors and they earn the lucrative incentive fees only if they perform.

| | S&P 500 | NASDAQ | Average U.S. Equity Mutual Fund Returns | Average U.S. Hedge Fund Returns |
|---|---|---|---|---|
| 2003: | +26.4% | +50.0% | | +15.4% |
| 2002: | −23.4% | −31.5% | | +3.0% |
| 2001: | −13.0% | −21.1% | +5.6% | +4.4% |
| 2000: | −10.1% | −39.3% | +8.0% | +4.9% |

*Source: Tremont Advisors*

## Why Start (or Work For) a Hedge Fund

1. **The limitless potential of the performance-based incentive fee structure.** The industry works on a "one and 20" formula, meaning the general partner earns a management fee of 1% of assets under administration and a performance fee equal to 20% of the fund's profits. (Compare that to the equity mutual fund industry norm, which is to only charge a management fee of between 2%–3%.)

So let's walk through an example in order to fully appreciate hedge fund economics.

Money manager XYZ raises $10 million to start his own hedge fund.

In year one, the firm earns $100,000 in management fees (1% of $10 million), which goes towards paying the expenses of the operation (office lease, Bloomberg terminal, etc.).

Let's assume the fund generated 15% returns. The 20% performance fee is calculated after the base management fee has been deducted, so:

Step 1: Calculate the fund's profits/returns
     15% x $9.9 million = $1,485,000

Step 2: Calculate the performance fee
     20% x $1,485,000 = $297,000

Now let's fast forward to year five and assume the fund's AUM have grown to $300 million and the manager has hired two analysts (one senior and one junior).

So in year five, the firm earns $3 million in management fees, of which $300,000 goes towards paying the salaries of the three professionals and the rest goes towards office expenses.

Let's assume that again, the fund generated 15% returns.

Step 1: Calculate the fund's profits/returns
     15% x $297 million = $44,550,000

Step 2: Calculate the performance fee
     20% x $44,550,000 = $8,910,000

and now the good part...

the junior analyst gets a bonus of $100,000

the senior analyst gets a bonus of $600,000

the fund manager gets what's left—$8,210,000!

And that, again, is on top of the $100,000 base salary! Now you see why successful hedge fund managers are at the very top of the Bay Street pecking order.

2. **The independence of building and running your own business**. There's a fair amount of marketing and client handholding in the process of gathering assets. However, if you put up good return numbers, the asset gathering tends to take care of itself.

3. **The freedom to invest in, or use, almost any financial instrument** (convertible bonds, derivatives [options, futures, and other financial instruments whose prices behave like the underlying stock/commodity], etc.) and any variety of investment techniques (short-selling [selling stock that one does not own with the expectation of making a profit by buying it back at a lower price], leverage [using borrowed funds to increase the amount invested in a position with the effect of magnifying the effects of small price movements], etc.) across a spectrum of investment styles to enhance risk-adjusted returns or control risk.

4. **The efficient use of time/resources**. The ability to short has practical considerations. Consider the following scenario: Traditional money managers and their analysts, who are almost exclusively long, may come across a potential investment idea and start to do the research. He or she reads the last couple annual reports, reads several sell-side research reports, talks to a few sell-side analysts who know the industry/company well, listens to the last several quarterly conference calls, etc. After several days of work, the manager/analyst concludes that the stock is overvalued at the current market price and

is likely heading lower. The manager/analyst then shelves the idea. A lot of work is left on the cutting room floor. A hedge fund manager, on the other hand, can act on that research and sell the stock short to take advantage of the declining stock price.

5. **Low barriers to entry for new funds.** In order to start a hedge fund in Canada, one simply has to be approved as an investment counsellor/portfolio manager by the Investment Dealers Association/ Ontario Securities Commission and have $35,000 in working capital.

## Hedge Fund Strategies

There are over a dozen hedge fund strategies in use. Here are the five most common ones, as per the Dow Jones Hedge Fund Strategy Benchmarks, and a sixth strategy that is common among Canadian funds.

### 1. Convertible Arbitrage

Convertible bonds are bonds that are convertible into shares of the issuing company's common stock. They generally carry a lower coupon rate than other corporate bonds of similar credit quality in exchange for the convertible feature. The attraction of convertible bonds is that the price of the bond falls less than the underlying stock in a declining market, but tends to track the price of the stock in a rising market. Convertible arbitrage strategies involve going long the bond and short the underlying stock of the same company to take advantage of pricing discrepancies. In Canada, there are a limited number of convertible bond issues and therefore this strategy is usually part of a multi-strategy fund.

## 2. Risk Arbitrage

Also referred to as merger arbitrage, funds that use this strategy try to generate positive returns by correctly anticipating the outcome of announced corporate takeovers or mergers. They buy the target company's stock and short the acquirer's stock. This strategy can be cyclical in that it is affected by the volume of merger and acquisition (M&A) deals, and in periods where there is little M&A deal flow there are a limited number of potential merger arbitrage situations.

## 3. Distressed Securities

Funds that play in this space buy the undervalued securities (or bank debt) of companies experiencing financial distress (bankruptcies and financial restructurings) or operational difficulties with the expectation that a successful turnaround/reorganization will materialize. Traditional money managers, due to portfolio guidelines/restrictions, cannot continue to hold securities of financially troubled companies. The artificial selling tends to exert abnormal selling pressure on the securities and cause an additional discount on the price beyond the fundamental reasons. Hedge funds capitalize on the mispricings of the securities as the company successfully reorganizes and attains higher valuations.

## 4. Event Driven

An event-driven strategy combines risk arbitrage and distressed securities investing, since the focus is to profit from company-specific events like mergers, acquisitions, bankruptcies, and financial restructurings.

### 5. Equity-Market Neutral (Nondirectional)

Positions in this type of portfolio consist of equal dollar amounts of long and offsetting short positions, thus "neutralizing" the market/systematic risk in the portfolio. The primary source of risk theoretically remaining in the portfolio is stock selection risk. Market-neutral managers buy the companies most likely to outperform and short the companies most likely to underperform in any given industry/sector. When unleveraged, this low volatility strategy is one of the more conservative on the hedge fund risk/reward spectrum.

### 6. Long/Short Equity (Directional)

Long/short fund managers tend to use a fundamental, bottom-up approach to selecting their long and short positions. Unlike market-neutral managers, however, long/short managers can be either net long or net short depending on their market view.

## A Day in the Life of a
## Top Hedge Fund Manager

Tom Schenkel, CFA, is a partner at hedge fund company Epic Capital Management. The firm's long/short directional equity hedge fund (Epic Canadian Long/Short Fund) was up 66% (before fees) in 2003.

Masters of Arts (economics) from Wilfrid Laurier University, 1994

Bachelor of Arts (economics) from Queen's University, 1992

I've been very fortunate in terms of my career on Bay Street in that I've worked with some of the best people out there. My first job was working as a research associate to a well-ranked mining analyst. After a year, I switched sectors and started working with one of the top-ranked consumer product analysts. In addition to developing industry and analytical expertise, working with such high-quality people taught me some of the more qualitative (but extremely important) aspects of the job: dedication, work ethic, and professionalism with clients.

After a total of three years as an associate, I was given primary coverage responsibilities on several industrial product companies. Shortly afterwards, I transitioned into a special situations role where I covered approximately 18 names in 12 different industry sectors. I believe the breadth of my coverage and therefore having to keep on top of so many names (and often their U.S. comparables) was great training for my current job.

After three years as a sell-side analyst, I began to understand some of the dynamics/trends relative to hedge funds in North America. We had relationships with some international hedge fund managers and after some initial discussions, realized that the penetration of hedge funds in Canada greatly lagged the levels of those in the United States. So our motivation for starting a hedge fund was twofold. First, there was a growing market opportunity in Canada to service clients who would want to diversify into an absolute return strategy. Second, we felt that our strong analytical backgrounds in complementary industry sectors and our combined 13 years of sell-side experience gave us the necessary skill set to manage money.

When we started the fund in November of 2000, we began with just a million dollars of assets under management, a substantial portion of which was our own money. Our goal was simple: to provide superior risk-adjusted returns. To do that, we employ a bottom-up, value-driven approach. We are very fundamentally oriented in our approach to stock selection. In our directional fund (the Canadian Long/Short Fund), we have now just exceeded $90 million in assets and will close the fund at $100 million. At that asset level, we feel we can continue to deliver absolute returns for our investors. As well, we manage a market-neutral fund called the North American Diversified Fund.

My typical day as a partner at a hedge fund company might look like this:

**5:45 a.m.**    My day starts.

**6:15 a.m.**    Review the news. Turn on CNBC and start to read through the Canadian financial newspapers. Then I check the online financial sources like WSJ.com and FT.com.

**7:30 a.m.**    Arrive at the office.

**7:35 a.m.**    Scan the news sources (e.g., Bloomberg), check morning research comments from brokers, look at how the overseas markets have done, and review our portfolio composition.

**8:30 a.m.**    Check my voicemail. There are several voicemails from the various salespeople that cover us.

**8:45 a.m.**    Get a call from my salesman at one of the global dealers. He is part of the group that is dedicated to covering hedge funds. I take the call because I don't hear from this salesman often but when he calls, he usually has a very good money-making idea.

**9:05 a.m.**    A base metals analyst from institutional boutique X calls to update me on his reasoning behind the changes in his commodity price forecasts and how they will affect the earnings estimates of the companies he covers. He highlights which of the mid-cap names have the most leverage to commodity price changes.

**9:17 a.m.**     I take a quick call from another salesperson reminding me about an initial public offering (IPO) that her firm is marketing and to arrange a one-on-one meeting between us and the company's senior management tomorrow.

**9:20 a.m.**     A rookie salesperson from bank-owned dealer Y calls to pitch his health care analyst's best long idea. I politely remind this salesperson (for the second—or is it third—time) that I tend not to go long biotech companies. Medical devices—yes. Mature pharmaceuticals—yes. But not biotech. We like to focus on sectors where we have a comparative advantage. On the long-side, biotech is not one of them.

**9:30 a.m.**     The market opens. I watch how the market opens, especially in terms of the names in our portfolio and the names we have on our "watch list."

**9:40 a.m.**     Bounce a couple ideas (prospective shorts) off of my partner. We agree to have one of our young analysts do research on the ideas.

**10:15 a.m.**    Earnings conference call.

**11:00 a.m.**    Meet with our two research analysts to review and refine ongoing research projects. We discuss some of the assumptions that they're using in their pro forma financial statements/models, go over the competitor names used in the comparative analysis, etc.

**12:00 p.m.**    My favorite sell-side analyst comes over and picks me up to go for a sandwich. It'll be a working lunch today.

**1:30 p.m.**     Back in the office just in time as the senior management team from steel company Z, accompanied by our salesman from broker B, shows up. One of our analysts and I meet with the management team.

**2:15 p.m.**     The management group leaves after a productive meeting.

**2:18 p.m.** Sit down with my analyst to compare notes. We're both impressed by the quality of the management team. They've differentiated themselves by having managed the company well through the trough of the cycle. (Good markets can mask the true performance of most companies— "a rising tide lifts all boats.")

**2:30 p.m.** Start making calls to steel industry contacts. Want to double-check the industry capacity utilization numbers that the company management just gave us. Would also like to know if there will be any significant capacity expansions in the next year.

**3:05 p.m.** Make calls to steel analysts on the sell-side. Want to compare the assumptions/calculations in our model to those of a couple of steel analysts that we trust.

**3:30 p.m.** Do some final number-crunching and comparative analysis on company Z before deciding that we should be long the stock.

**3:48 p.m.** Call the salesperson at broker B to place a buy order for company Z stock, since he was the one that first gave us the idea and he also arranged the management meeting. I give him an order to buy us a starting position in steel company Z.

**4:00 p.m.** Market closes.

**4:05 p.m.** Sit down with our CFO to review business issues and any administrative matters.

**5:00 p.m.** Head off to the gym for a workout and a game of squash with one of my former sell-side colleagues.

**6:30 p.m.** Meet for drinks with a hedge fund-of-funds manager who is contemplating increasing his allocation to our fund.

**7:30 p.m.** Back at the office. This is a good time to revisit the prospective short ideas that I delegated.

**8:00 p.m.** Time to do some general business reading, so I grab a copy of the latest issues of *The Economist* and *BusinessWeek*, and a sell-side industry research piece.

# HOW HEDGE FUND MANAGERS SPEND THEIR TIME

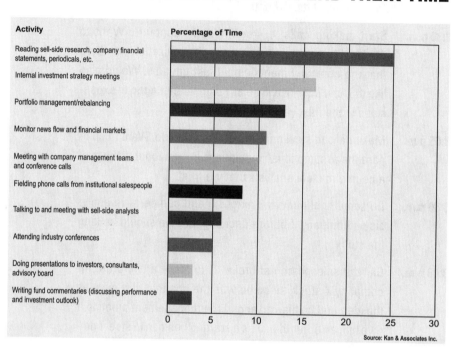

| Activity | Percentage of Time |
|---|---|

Reading sell-side research, company financial statements, periodicals, etc.

Internal investment strategy meetings

Portfolio management/rebalancing

Monitor news flow and financial markets

Meeting with company management teams and conference calls

Fielding phone calls from institutional salespeople

Talking to and meeting with sell-side analysts

Attending industry conferences

Doing presentations to investors, consultants, advisory board

Writing fund commentaries (discussing performance and investment outlook)

0   5   10   15   20   25   30

Source: Kan & Associates Inc.

## A Chat with a Hedge Fund-of-Funds Manager

**Jim McGovern** is managing director and chief executive officer of Arrow Hedge Partners Inc. Prior to joining Arrow Hedge Partners, he co-founded mutual fund company BPI and 14 years later sold the company to CI Funds.

**Q. How did you get started in the hedge fund business?**

**A.** In 1995 we were approached by John Reinsberg and Michael Rome of Lazard Frères Asset Management in New

York City to distribute a global long/short fund in Canada. We worked for a long time with our legal advisors and the dealer community to create the first weekly priced hedge fund. It was nationally distributed on the FundServ platform. The Fund performed exceedingly well and we were on our way to managing over $500 million in similar strategies by 1999.

**Q. What is the concept behind Arrow Hedge Partners Inc.?**

A. Arrow Hedge Partners Inc. is a Canadian-based company specializing in hedge funds. Our three core values are focus (we only manage/distribute hedge funds), risk management (hedge funds that are focused on capital preservation), and integrity (we are the largest investors in our own funds, principals have a long history in the business, etc.). The company is focused on being the preeminent alternative investment firm in Canada with research and distribution globally.

**Q. Given that Arrow Hedge offers both a fund-of-funds product and a single manager product, what are the pros and cons of each?**

A. Advisors and their clients have different investment requirements over time. Our "single manager" offerings are focused on specialized long/short strategies (global, Canadian, Asian, etc.) and are ideal complements to traditional equity portfolios. They essentially substitute equity risk for active manager risk (or selling beta to get more alpha). The cons with any single manager are the non-systematic or operational risks—these can be effectively diversified away with a fund of hedge funds (FOFs). FOFs provide effective diversification, professional management, administrative ease, and often superior liquidity. The biggest drawback is the extra cost/fees of hiring an FOF manager.

**Q. How does Arrow Hedge differentiate its products relative to other FOF managers?**

A. Arrow differentiates itself in a number of ways. In our "core" Multi-Strategy product we will allocate to all the principal hedge fund strategies, including those such as global macro or long/short equity, which are not necessarily market neutral. As a result we will have beta (market directionality), albeit at low levels, in our Fund. We are very diversified, with over 20 managers from around the globe contributing to the portfolio. Outside of portfolio construction our three key differentials are transparency, low fees, and good liquidity. With all our managers we have 100% position-level transparency and can review all trading activity. We have an extremely low additional cost over and above our underlying hedge fund managers. And finally, investors access their capital (i.e., redeem) on very reasonable terms (generally monthly with short notice).

**Q. Could you tell us about the Alternative Investment Management Association?**

A. The Alternative Investment Management Association (AIMA) was established in 1990 in the UK as a non-profit organization for the alternative investment industry. It specifically includes hedge funds, managed futures, and managed currency funds.

AIMA's objectives are to:

- increase investor education, improve transparency, and promote due diligence and related best practices

- work closely with regulators and interested parties in order to better promote and control the use of alternative investments

Local industry participants formed the Canadian chapter of AIMA in 2003. From an original membership of 38,

AIMA Canada had grown to 54 members by the end of March 2004. In addition to an Executive Committee, AIMA Canada has four working subcommittees including Legal & Regulatory, Events, Education & Research, and Tax & Finance to implement its objectives.

**Q.** **In the U.S. there are about 6,000 hedge funds. Using the typical 10-to-1 ratio when comparing U.S. versus Canada statistics, we should have close to 600 hedge funds on this side of the border yet there are only 30. How do you explain the difference in the penetration levels of hedge funds in the two countries?**

**A.** Canada typically lags the U.S. in terms of adoption of financial products, often by five to 10 years. This was the case in terms of mutual funds in the '80s and now hedge funds in the '90s. There are a number of reasons. Canadian investors are often more conservative than their U.S. counterparts. Secondly, there are more managers based in the U.S. and greater demand for product specialization as a result of a more sophisticated investment marketplace. Thirdly, there are more "wealthy" (therefore "accredited") investors per capita in the U.S.

**Q.** **What are the current themes/trends in alternative investments in Canada?**

**A.** Within the institutional marketplace a great deal of focus has been made on educating plan sponsors and trustees about the benefits and drawbacks of alternative funds and how they can play a role in the institutional portfolio. While major sponsors such as Ontario Teachers and the Caisse de dépôt et placement du Québec (CDPQ) have been active for a long time in the area, other large- and medium-size plans have started allocating to FOFs. In the retail/high-net-worth marketplace, structured products (featuring capital guarantees and low minimum investments) have been enormously popular with investors.

**Q. With more institutional money flowing into alternative investments, has there been a push for more transparency and accountability?**

A. Without a doubt, the push towards transparency and accountability has been generated by institutional investors. As fiduciaries, they are focused on "process" and how returns are generated (or not), so these issues are paramount. There has been a great deal of debate recently as to the importance of transparency. On the one hand, recent high-profile problems such as Lancer and Beacon Hill make institutions more wary of hedge funds, while on the other hand, hedge fund managers are loathe to give out their holdings as it may prejudice their trading position (and cost them returns). The delicate balance is probably best struck with something called "risk transparency" whereby a bona fide third party provides the institution with details on items like concentration, geographic breakdowns, number of positions, position sizes, value-added-risk (VAR), etc. on a regular basis in lieu of full-position-level transparency.

**Q. Hedge funds in Canada have capped their funds (in terms of asset size), some as low as $100 million. What's the reasoning behind capping the fund? Is there an optimum fund size?**

A. Hedge fund managers only cap their funds when they feel that the economics of trading larger sums of capital diminish, that is, there is an optimum size at which point generating performance fees will suffer if that level is breached. For example, managers skilled as stock pickers focusing on small-cap Canadian stocks would want to remain small so that they could trade around their positions without impacting the market. Depending on the strategy employed and the markets traded, there is clearly a wide range of capacity limits ranging from $100 million to several billion dollars. Capping of assets is in the interests of all parties—investors and manager.

**Q. Which investment style is currently the most common among hedge funds in Canada?**

A. At this stage the most common investment style is long/short equity.

**Q. What backgrounds/skill sets do you find most common among successful hedge fund managers?**

A. Most hedge fund managers are either experienced long-only managers (mutual or pension fund managers or strategists) or highly ranked sell-side analysts. Hedge fund managers are also often ex-proprietary ("prop") traders at banks or major financial institutions, or former hedge fund managers at larger funds striking out on their own. The key skill is their competitive advantage or edge over other managers/traders in the market. They may have unique insights or expertise on an industry, geographic region, quantitative model, etc. that makes them valuable (i.e., profitable) in the marketplace. Overall, skill-based strategies require an enormous dedication by managers to their fund to stay on top of their game. Tenacity, intelligence, street smarts, experience, business savvy, and personal commitment are just a few of the key traits.

**Q. How do you go about selecting managers for your products?**

A. We select hedge fund managers for our products based on rigorous upfront and continuing due diligence. The due diligence is both quantitatively and qualitatively focused, with greater emphasis placed on the latter. The initial due diligence is focused on verifying and analyzing the manager's credentials and skill in their chosen strategy. This is accomplished by on-site visits, extensive reference and industry checks, and a thorough review of the manager's track record.

**Q. What piece of advice would you want to pass on to people aspiring to join/start a hedge fund?**

A. If you are aspiring to join or start a hedge fund, my key piece of advice would be to get good advice! Most hedge fund failures are the result of operational-type issues, the most important of which is to understand that you are running a business and a hedge fund. You should ensure that you have solid counterparties—legal, accounting, prime brokerage, and administration partners are critical. You should also avail yourself of the great reference sources in the marketplace including AIMA Canada's recently released *Guide to Sound Practices for Canadian Hedge Fund Managers* (March 2004).

## Comparing a Hedge Fund Manager with a Mutual Fund Manager

|  | Hedge Fund Manager | Mutual Fund Manager |
|---|---|---|
| Business model | Performance game—fees tied primarily to performance | Volume business— fees tied to AUM |
| Definition of risk | Potential loss of invested capital | Deviation from a stated benchmark |
| Return objective | Absolute returns—positive returns in all market conditions | Relative returns— returns above a related benchmark |

| | Hedge Fund Manager | Mutual Fund Manager |
|---|---|---|
| Performance measurement | Peer-group comparisons | Use of benchmarks |
| Upper range of total compensation | Multi-millions | Multi-millions |
| Transparency in disclosure | Lightly regulated | Highly regulated |
| Ability to sell short | Yes | No |
| Ability to use leverage | Yes | No |
| Ability to use derivatives | Yes | No |
| Intellectual freedom | High—wide range of investment tools/strategies | Low—long positions only |
| Management fees | 1%–2% | 2%–3% |
| Performance fees | 20% of fund's profits | None |
| Interests aligned with investors | Bulk of personal money invested in the fund | Little, if any, personal wealth invested in the fund |
| Upside in bull markets | High absolute returns = high performance fees | Good relative returns = good performance bonuses |
| Downside in bear markets | Low absolute returns = low performance fees | Poor relative returns = low, or no, performance bonuses |

## Suggested Reading

1. *Absolute Returns: The Risk and Opportunities of Hedge Fund Investing* (by Alexander M. Ineichen, published by John Wiley & Sons)

   Written by the Head of Equity Derivatives Research of UBS Warburg in London, this comprehensive guide is written for the professional investor.

2. *Adventure Capitalist: The Ultimate Road Trip* (by Jim Rogers, published by Random House)

   This is Rogers' second round-the-world trip—three years, 116 countries.

3. *Confessions of a Street Addict* (by James J. Cramer, published by Simon & Schuster)

   The co-founder of TheStreet.com and former hedge fund manager gives the reader a peek at how the Wall Street game is really played.

4. *Convertible Arbitrage: Insights and Techniques for Successful Hedging* (by Nick P. Calamos, published by John Wiley & Sons)

   Written by a successful convertible bond manager, this book provides practical and detailed information on one of the more common hedge fund strategies.

5. *Evaluating and Implementing Hedge Fund Strategies: The Experience of Managers and Investors—3rd Edition* (by Ronald Lake, published by Euromoney Books)

   Written by practitioners in the field, this guide provides a thorough discussion of the various hedge fund investment techniques.

6. *The Handbook of Alternative Investments* (edited by Darrell Jobman, published by John Wiley & Sons)

   This is a contributed volume where each contributor lends insights into the various investments (hedge funds, real estate, private equity, etc.) whose returns are uncorrelated to traditional stock and bond returns.

7. *Hedge Funds: Definitive Strategies and Techniques* (edited by IMCA, Kenneth S. Phillips, and Ronald J. Surz, published by John Wiley & Sons)

   Simply what the title suggests—another good hedge fund primer.

8. *Investing in Hedge Funds* (by Joseph G. Nicholas, published by Bloomberg Press)

   This is a good resource for readers who want a good hedge fund primer that discusses hedge fund basics and then clearly outlines the various hedge fund strategies.

9. *Investment Biker: Around the World With Jim Rogers* (by Jim Rogers, published by Random House)

   Written by the man *Time* magazine calls "the Indiana Jones of finance," *Investment Biker* recounts the 20-month and 52-country motorcycle odyssey/investing trip taken by Jim Rogers, the co-founder of the Quantum Fund with George Soros.

10. *Managing a Hedge Fund: A Complete Guide to Trading, Business Strategies, Operations, and Regulations* (by Keith H. Black, published by McGraw-Hill)

For those interested in starting their own hedge fund, this book provides information on most business and investing issues facing a start-up fund manager.

11. *Market-Neutral Investing: Long/Short Hedge Fund Strategies* (by Joseph G. Nicholas, published by Bloomberg Press)

The author (founder and chairman of Hedge Fund Research Inc.) uses non-technical language in his discussion of market-neutral strategies and how to put together a market-neutral portfolio.

12. *Soros on Soros: Staying Ahead of the Curve* (by George Soros, published by John Wiley & Sons)

This is a book-length interview into the life and mind of one of the legendary investors of our time. Soros shares his thoughts on more than just investing; the reader also gets insight into his views on politics, philosophy, and philanthropy.

13. *When Genius Failed: The Rise and Fall of Long-Term Capital Management* (by Roger Lowenstein, published by Random House)

This is a riveting account of John Meriwether (ex-Salomon Brothers superstar bond trader) and his cast of elite financial economists (including two Nobel Prize winners) whose over-reliance on their complex financial models to predict market behaviour, and their extreme use of leverage, brought down the world's largest hedge fund, which in turn threatened to collapse the financial system.